D1377287

LARGEMOUTH BASS

© Wally Eberhart

LARGEMOUTH BASS

TIMOTHY FREW

MALLARD PRESS
An imprint of BDD Promotional Book Company, Inc.
666 Fifth Avenue
New York, New York 10103

A FRIEDMAN GROUP BOOK

Published by MALLARD PRESS
An imprint of BDD Promotional Book Company, Inc.
666 Fifth Avenue
New York, New York 10103

Mallard Press and its accompanying design and logo are trademarks of BDD Promotional Book Company, Inc.

First published in the United States of America in 1991 by The Mallard Press.

ISBN 0-792-45292-5

LARGEMOUTH BASS: An Angler's Guide
was prepared and produced by
Michael Friedman Publishing Group, Inc.
15 West 26th Street
New York, New York 10010

Editor: Melissa Schwarz
Art Director: Jeff Batzli
Designer: Susan Livingston
Photo Researcher: Daniella Jo Nilva

Typeset by: EAC/Interface
Color separations by Universal Colour Scanning, Ltd.
Printed and bound in Hong Kong by Leefung-Asco Printers Limited

Dedication

This book is dedicated to the memories of my grandparents Harry and Helen Frew and Ira and Mildred Brown and the many enjoyable summers spent with them at Crystal Beach and Red Point.

Acknowledgements

I would like to thank the many editors that had a hand in this book: Sharon Kalman, who signed me up; Melissa Schwarz, who took over the project, and Liz Sullivan who finished the job. I would also like to thank Sue Livingston, the designer, for the final look of the book and for patiently complying with my many changes and Daniella Jo Nilva for acquiring the many fine photographs.

TABLE OF CONTENTS

© Wally Eberhart

INTRODUCTION

The largemouth bass is a hearty warm-water fish known for its explosive strikes on surface lures and its tenacity in weed beds. In many areas in the United States, the largemouth bass is virtually synonymous

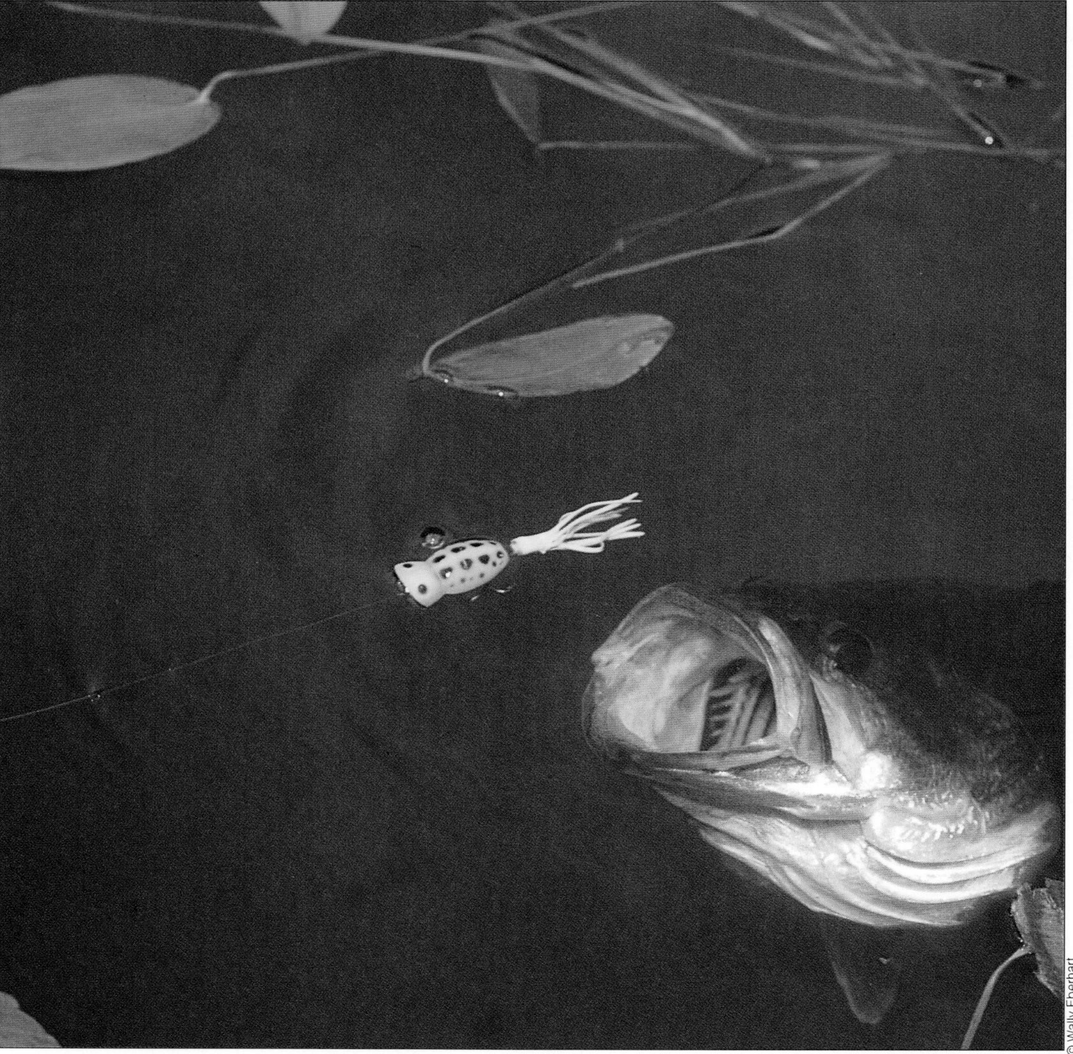

A hungry largemouth opens up and prepares to inhale a surface lure. Much of the largemouth's popularity comes from the fact that it will readily hit artificial lures.

© Wally Eberhart

with freshwater fishing. The fish has inspired yearly bass-fishing championships, affectionately known as bass wars, where expert anglers gather to see who pulls in the biggest lunker. Difficult to find, yet often eager to fight, the largemouth bass has become one of the most popular game fish in all of North America. Every year, anglers armed with the latest in bait-casting equipment, high-powered boats, and sensitive electronic equipment descend upon bass-laden lakes and reservoirs in hopes of doing battle with these age-old competitors.

Every experienced bass angler has a favorite lure that he or she "guarantees" will pull in the most bass. Some bass anglers fish for sheer numbers, while others concentrate on searching out only the oldest and largest fish in the water. Many anglers go back to the same hole year after year to try to pull out that large bass they always see under the same lily pad.

While not as widespread as its larger-mouthed cousin, the smallmouth bass, too, has become a highly sought after fish in North America. Found in slightly cooler, faster-moving waters, the smallmouth bass has gained a reputation for being a strong, determined fighter. In fact, many anglers who fish for both prefer the smallmouth bass for its hard strikes and long runs.

Bass anglers across the country argue incessantly over the best methods for catching these freshwater denizens. Some say that a quickly fished spoon will pull in the most bass, while others maintain that only a Texas-rigged plastic worm is consistently deadly. There are almost as many fishing techniques for these fish as there are bass anglers on a busy lake. The only surefire way to learn how to catch bass is to hop on a boat and fish for them. This book does, however, give you several suggestions to keep in mind when you go out on that much-anticipated fishing vacation. Covered here are spawning

Fly fishing for smallmouth bass is an extremely challenging and exciting sport. Pound for pound, smallmouth bass fight as hard as any freshwater game fish in North America.

habits, feeding characteristics, pointers on locating the fish, and several popular angling methods for a variety of fishing situations.

While this book concentrates mostly on largemouth and smallmouth bass, it also includes chapters devoted to two lesser varieties of bass that have experienced a sharp increase in angling popularity over the past several years: the striped bass and the white bass. These two bass are an enjoyable catch for all anglers, but are particularly good fish for beginners to fish for as they are not particularly difficult to catch yet offer quite a bit of angling excitement.

If you have never fished for bass before, there is no time like the present to start. At a time when salmon, trout, and other popular game are suffering from the strains of pollution and overfishing, largemouth, smallmouth, striped, and white bass can be found in record numbers. In fact, some areas have increased their bag limits over recent years to help stem burgeoning populations of these prolific fish. So, hop on a boat, rig up line, and take part in the increasing bass boom.

Chapter 1

© Hanson Carroll/FPG International

LARGEMOUTH BASICS

The largemouth bass, or *Micropterus salmoides,* is one of the most sought after game fish in North America. Its adaptability, eagerness to feed, love of cover, and fighting ability have endeared it to anglers

***Micropterus salmoides** gets its common name from its extremely large mouth that extends beyond the back edge of its eye. Another obvious identifying characteristic is the fish's dark lateral stripe.*

for hundreds of years. Like its close cousins the smallmouth and the spotted bass, the largemouth is a member of a group known as black bass, which is part of the sunfish family.

The largemouth's natural range runs from southern Ontario through the Great Lakes and the Mississippi river system, and along the coastal plain from North Carolina to northeast Mexico. Because it is easy to breed, tolerant of a variety of water temperatures, and able to survive in a wide assortment of aquatic environments, the largemouth has become a favorite with hatchery and stocking programs. In fact, this bass is the most widely stocked fish in North America. Today, largemouth populations can be found in every state in the continental United States as well as throughout most of southern Canada. It has also been introduced in Europe, Asia, Africa, and South America.

Other common names for the *Micropterus salmoides* include bigmouth bass, green bass, green trout, lake bass, mossback, and linesides. The most popular name for this game fish comes from its extremely large mouth which extends past the back edge of the eye. In addition, the hooked lower jaw sticks out beyond the upper jaw. The largemouth has a drab olive to dark green back and a creamy white to gray belly. Its sides are greenish yellow with a dark lateral stripe. As the largemouth gets older it turns darker and its markings fade. As with most other fish, however, the male largemouth's markings become more prominent around spawning time.

The size of the largemouth depends on such factors as fish populations, water temperatures, and the abundance of food. In lakes where there are

a lot of bass, fish tend to be smaller because they must compete for food. Also, if waters are cool through much of the year, the feeding and growing season is much shorter and bass are smaller. In northern lakes, largemouth bass usually weigh from 1 to 5 pounds (.5 to 2.3 kg), with a 6 or 7 pounder (2.7 or 3 kg) considered a trophy fish. In the South, where the feeding and growing season is much longer, larger fish are more common. In Florida especially, 8 to 10 pounders (3.6 to 4.5 kg) can be quite common. In southern waters, bass grow much faster than in the North; however, they tend not to live as long. Southern bass live a maximum of ten years, while northern bass quite often live fifteen years or longer. The rod-and-reel record for the largemouth is 22 pounds (10 kg), 4 ounces (112 g), caught by George Perry in Montgomery Lake, Georgia, on June 2, 1932.

The largemouth's large mouth combined with a flexible stomach allows it to quickly inhale fairly sizeable prey. The fish opens its mouth and sucks in its quarry and the surrounding water. It then expels the water through its gills and either swallows or spits out the food. This whole process takes only a second or two, making the job of setting the hook quite challenging for the angler. While the largemouth will eat almost anything, its favorite foods seem to be frogs, salamanders, shiners, and crawfish. In addition to its sense of taste, the largemouth relies primarily on touch when deciding whether to swallow or reject a piece of food. If an object feels hard and artificial, the fish will reject it quickly; if it feels soft and natural, the bass will hold onto it a bit longer. This is one of the reasons why plastic worms are one of the most effective baits against the largemouth.

The black lateral line is actually a series of sensitive nerve endings that help the fish to sense even the most subtle underwater vibrations. Part of the reason why spinner baits are effective in catching largemouths is that they send off vibrations similar to those of a bait fish.

© Wally Eberhart

Ichthyologists divide the largemouth into two subspecies, the Florida largemouth and the northern largemouth. Originally the Florida bass was found only in the warm Florida water system; however, this larger strain has been successfully transplanted throughout the South. Pure strains of Florida bass are becoming increasingly rare as these fish hybridize with the northern bass. The world record bass caught by George Perry is believed to have been a Florida/northern hybrid. For most anglers, the distinction between largemouth strains is unimportant.

SENSES

All bass have a black lateral line that runs from the head to tail on either side of the fish. This lateral line is not just distinctive, but contains a series of nerve endings. It can pick up even subtle underwater vibrations that warn the fish of danger or alert it to the presence of bait fish. Even in the dead of night in murky water, a largemouth bass can sense the presence of bait fish and other food through its lateral line.

The largemouth will use its sense of touch to decide whether or not to swallow. If the object feels unnatural in the bass's mouth, the fish will quickly spit it out.

© Wally Eberhart

Bass have fairly good eyesight for freshwater fish. They can see in all directions except directly behind or below themselves. Their eyesight is good enough to see objects on or above the water. If you bring your boat too close to a bass or if you sit too high in your seat, you may startle the fish and ruin your luck. Even though visibility in most bass waters is limited to 5 to 8 feet (1.5 to 2.5 m), bass have a visual range of up to 30 feet (9 m). In addition, the largemouth's eyes are very sensitive to light. The fish will stay in shady areas as much as possible, especially on sunny days.

Many anglers believe that bass prefer certain colors over others. While biologists have determined that the fish can distinguish color, nothing about color preferences in bass has ever been proven. The action of a lure is much more important than its color.

Largemouth bass have internal ears located within their skulls. Along with the lateral line, these ears are very good at picking up the noise and vibrations of bait fish and other quarry. These same senses also attract the largemouth bass to the popping and chugging noise of the angler's surface lure. In recent years anglers have been experimenting with sonic lures to attract bass.

The bass uses its sense of smell and taste when deciding whether or not to swallow something it has caught in its mouth. The fish's huge mouth is lined with sensitive taste-buds on both the inside and outside of the lips. The fish smells through short passageways called nares on its snout. These nares enable the fish to draw in and expel water without the water entering its throat. While the bass does have excellent senses of smell and taste, it depends more on the way an object feels when deciding whether or not to swallow it.

During the spring and fall, largemouth bass will do most of their feeding in the shallow areas of lakes and rivers. Look for them along craggy bottoms, in lily beds, and around fallen trees or rocks.

SPAWNING

In the early spring, just as the waters begin to warm up, largemouth bass shake off their winter dormancy and begin feeding voraciously in preparation for their spring spawning. The exact spawning time for the largemouth is directly related to water temperatures. Bass will not spawn until the inshore waters reach at least 60°F (16°C). A late winter can delay spawning until late April or early May. On the other hand, if a warm front raises the water temperature above 70°F (21°C), largemouths hold off or interrupt the spawning process for as long as two months, until the water cools again.

Largemouth bass spawn in a wide variety of freshwater habitats. As the water warms, they move into shallow bays, backwaters, inlets, channels, and other areas that are protected from strong currents and prevailing winds. Most bass choose spawning grounds with firm sandy or gravelly bottoms; however, they sometimes spawn in areas with a lot of mud or rock. The male bass spends several days selecting the perfect spot to

Young bass fingerlings are the favorite food of many aquatic predators. Most fingerlings will never reach spawning age themselves. In fact, out of the 2,000 to 10,000 eggs in an average nest, only about 5 fry will survive long enough to reach 10 inches (25 cm) in length.

build the nest. This spot is usually within 10 feet (3 m) of shore and in depths ranging from 1 to 6 feet (.3 to 2 m). The male chooses a site that is easy to defend, near a pocket of bulrushes, next to a sunken log or a boulder, and within easy access to deep water. In addition, the male will not build a nest within 30 feet (9 m) of another visible spawning nest. Occasionally, bass nests will be closer together, but only if they are not in a direct visual line with each other.

After choosing a site, the male begins digging into the bottom with wide sweeps of its tail. It clears away all debris and digs a nest a few inches deep and about a foot wide (the width of the nest depends on the size of the fish). Then, if the water temperature is between 63° and 68°F (17° and 20°C), the female hovers over the nest and deposits her eggs. The female bass lays anywhere from 2,000 to 7,000 eggs for every pound of body weight. She may deposit her eggs in one nest or spread them out into several nests at different times before leaving the spawning area. Once her egg supply is depleted, the female moves into deeper water to recuperate for about two or three weeks. During the spawning and recuperation period, neither the female nor the male eats.

Once the female releases her eggs, the male takes position above the nest and deposits his milt, spreading it over the eggs with gentle sweeps of his tail. Occasionally several males deposit milt in the same nest; however, only the dominant male remains to guard the young.

Bass eggs and young fry are favorite meals of bluegills, salamanders, sunfish, crawfish, and a variety of other aquatic predators. For any of the eggs to have a chance of survival, the male bass must remain over the nest and keep a vigilant eye on it until several days after the eggs hatch. The male does not eat while guarding the nest, but he will attack any fish venturing into the area. If it is a slow-moving predator such as a crawfish, the bass will simply pick

© Robert A. Walsh

it up and move it out of the way. Schools of bluegills and sunfish are a particular threat to bass. They will swarm around a net, and while the bass chases one fish away, others will raid the nest from the rear.

The incubation period for bass eggs depends on water temperature. At 68°F (20°C), the eggs will hatch in about five days; if the temperature goes above 70°F (21°C) they may hatch in as little as two days. A sudden cold spell can be devastating to the eggs. If the water temperature drops below 50°F (10°C), the male leaves the nest and the eggs are quickly devoured by predators.

The tiny bass fry remain in the nest until their yolk sacs are absorbed. They then move into a heavy weed bed or other shallow water cover. Once the fry leave the nest, the male bass moves to deeper water, where he lies suspended for several days until he has completely recuperated. For their first few weeks away from the nest, the tiny fry feed on plankton until they reach a length of 2 inches (5 cm). As they continue to grow, their diet gradually shifts to insects and then small fish. Young bass fry are a transparent yellow with a thin black stripe down each side. As with many other types of fish, bass have a high attrition rate. Out of the 2,000 to 10,000 eggs that hatch from the average nest, only about 5 fry will survive long enough to reach 10 inches (25 cm) in length.

Largemouth bass can be found anywhere from a small pond to a large lake, as long as the water has plenty of oxygen, maintains a warm temperature, and there is a lot of structure below the body of water's surface.

© Bob Firth/Firth Photobank

HABITAT

Bass are very adaptable and can survive in a wide variety of conditions that would wipe out most other game fish. Healthy largemouths have been found in small stagnant ponds, manmade reservoirs, large natural lakes, and wide, slow-moving rivers. In *Fishing with Ray Bergman*, the venerated angling expert wrote about how several bass were put in a rearing pond that was later allowed to go dry in the fall. The pond was nothing more than a muddy depression until the spring when it gradually filled with rain water. Small shad fry were stocked in the pond, but hatchery officials soon noticed that some sort of large fish was feeding on the small shad. Those large fish turned out to be bass. Apparently, when the pond began to go dry in the fall, the bass dug their way into the mud and remained there in dormancy until spring, when the pond filled back up again.

Even though bass do possess a remarkable knack for survival, there are still several factors essential to good bass waters. Bass require more oxygen than most other types of

game fish. Almost all lakes have adequate oxygen levels in their shallows; however, many "fertile" lakes—those with high nutrient levels—may lack sufficient oxygen in the deeper regions. Because of their high nutrient levels, fertile lakes produce a great deal of plankton and algae. These tiny organisms eventually die and sink to the bottom. As these organisms decompose, they consume large amounts of oxygen, making the lake's depths unsuitable for most fish. This is a particular problem when raw sewage is either dumped or leaked into a lake. The sewage adds too many nutrients to the water, making the lake overfertile.

Many fertile lakes in the north suffer from a phenomenon known as winter kill. In these lakes, ice and snow block out enough sunlight to slow the photosynthesis of aquatic plants. As a result, not enough oxygen is produced in the water, making it inhospitable to higher aquatic life forms. Because bass require relatively high oxygen levels, they are usually the first to die out.

© Jim P. Garrison

Left: ***A largemouth is pulled from a weed bed after being hooked with a spinner bait.*** **Right:** ***Thick weed beds are favorite hiding spots of the largemouth bass. They will hold in the midst of these thick beds, and wait for a bait fish to swim by.***

Water temperature is also very important to the survival of the largemouth. The warmer the waters, the more bass will feed and grow. During the winter, when the water temperatures are below 50°F (10°C), bass eat very little, if at all. As the water warms to between 50° and 68°F (10° and 20°C), feeding gradually increases. The largemouth's metabolism is at its peak in waters between 68° and 80°F (20° and 27°C). They will be very active and sometimes careless in their relentless pursuit of food, often striking at objects that don't even resemble any type of natural food. This is the best time for fishing the largemouth. Occasionally, however, bass will abandon waters in the optimal temperature range in order to escape bright sunlight. If water temperatures rise above 80°F (27°C), feeding begins to decline and the fish become slow and lethargic. In water above 95°F (35°C), bass die out.

If there is one truth about the largemouth bass, it is that this fish really loves structure. Structure is any feature that offers variety in the bass's underwater habitat. It includes permanent, topographical features such as old, submerged creek beds, rocky ledges, drop-offs, submerged islands, points, crags, and shoals.

More transitory underwater features are also categorized as structure. These include weed beds, brush piles, logs, stumps, rock piles, sandbars, and logjams. Thick weed beds are favorite hiding spots of the largemouth bass. Big lunkers love to hold over or in the midst of thick weeds, waiting for an unsuspecting minnow or crawfish to happen by. While weed beds can be difficult to fish, they are often the most productive spots for really big largemouths.

From the moment they are hatched, largemouth bass head immediately into thick weed beds and

© M. Timothy O'Keefe/Tom Stack & Associates

One universal truth about the largemouth bass is that it loves to hold in and around underwater structure. Weed beds, fallen trees, rocks, and brush all serve as hiding places for these elusive fish.

© Wally Eberhart

around sunken logs and rock piles for protection from predators. Bass retain this instinct to hide even after they are full grown, despite the fact that they have few natural enemies. They use weeds, rocks, flooded timber, and brush and other objects for shade, shelter, and ambush points.

One interesting characteristic of the bass is that if there are many different types of structure in an area, the bass will often be using only one type at any given time. This can be as obvious as a bridge piling or as subtle as a spot where the light varies or the water temperature shifts. In *The Compleat Freshwater Fisherman*, the writers for the Hunting and Fishing Library write about an experiment conducted with largemouth bass in a tank. In a plain white tank where the light is evenly distributed, this fish became confused, often swimming about aimlessly. When a board was placed over one edge of the tank, creating a shady spot in the water, the bass immediately gathered in the shade. Next the board was removed and a pile of rocks was added. The fish quickly gathered around the rocks. In the final experiment the bass were put in a tank that contained no cover, but had a black stripe painted on the side. Even though it offered no protection, the bass hovered near the stripe, the varying element in the tank environment.

Many of the most productive largemouth waters are man-made lakes or reservoirs. Bass thrive in these clean structure-filled impoundments. Quite often these reservoirs will have a submerged river- or creek-

This netted largemouth went after a plastic worm, the most popular of all largemouth lures.

bed. Reservoirs are constructed by damming a river or creek. As the surrounding area floods, the creek bed often remains intact in a deep section of the lake. With a multitude of curves, bends, drop-offs, and pools, old creek beds offer prime bass structure. Bass also tend to follow old river- and creek-beds as guides when they migrate through reservoirs.

In addition to river- and creek-beds, reservoirs usually contain acres of old stump fields. Before the reservoir is flooded, most of the trees in what would become shallow water areas are cut down. If you can locate one of these old stump fields, you may be in for some exciting fishing. Other types of structure present in most reservoirs include old road beds, bridge pilings, brush piles, and sometimes old construction shacks or even entire houses.

Most experienced bass anglers have become experts at reading topographical maps. These maps are invaluable when fishing unknown bass waters. Electronic depthfinders are also invaluable tools for searching out largemouth bass in deep structure. The more experience you gain as an angler, the better you will become at reading the bottoms of lakes and reservoirs and finding the spots where the prime bass are hiding. There is an old saying about bass fishing that goes something like this: "You may find structure without bass, but you will never find bass too far from structure."

© Robert A. Walsh

Chapter 2

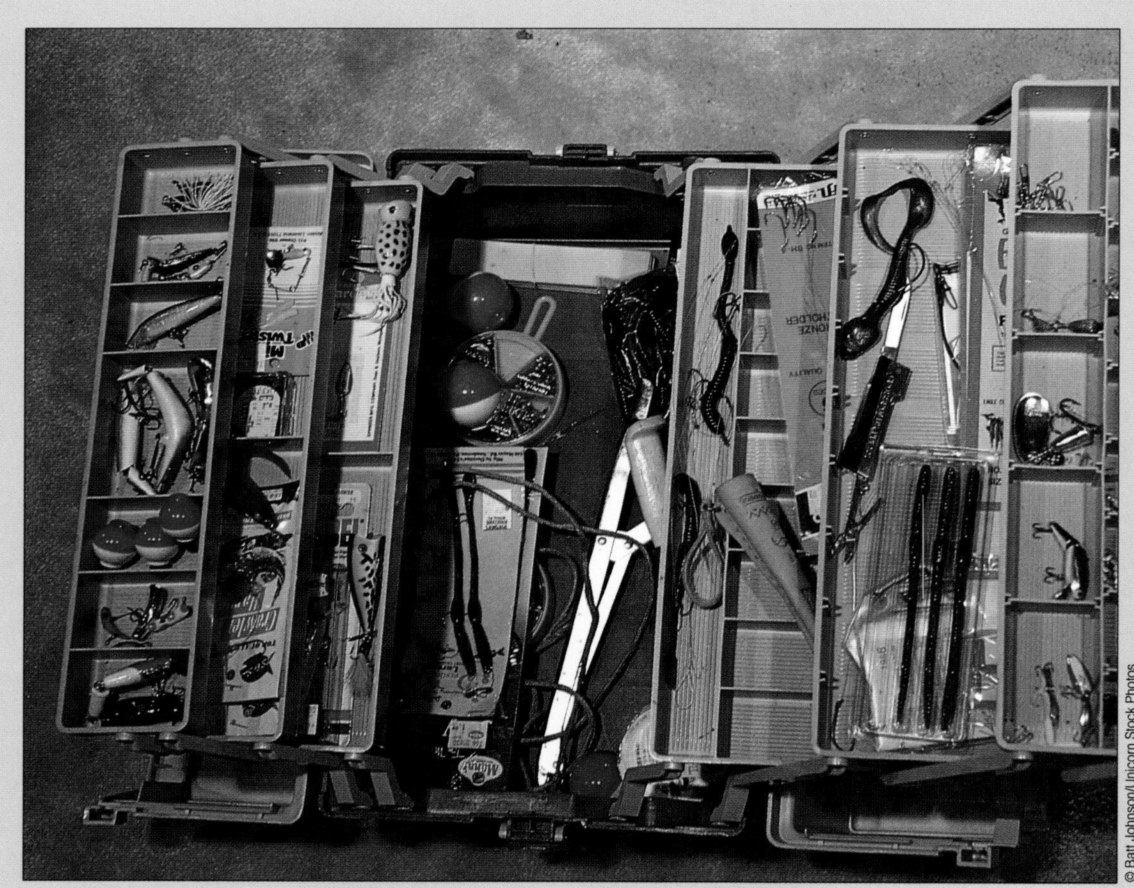

Bass Busters: Lures and Baits

The largemouth bass is a ravenous eater as its name may imply. A young bass will go after a wide variety of quarry—from frogs to salamanders to minnows to bluegills. As the fish grows older and wiser, however, it will

© Hanson Carroll/FPG International

become much more selective in its eating habits; such is the challenge of catching an old lunker. The largemouth is relatively high in the freshwater aquatic food chain and has very few enemies other than man. In addition, it is a very territorial fish that is easily angered and provoked to attack.

Bass anglers with any experience at all are well acquainted with the fish's readiness to take an artificial lure. Whether out of hunger, curiosity, or anger, a largemouth will eagerly strike a lure that does not resemble any type of natural food. In fact, many highly successful bass lures look more like metallic airplane propellers than any kind of live bait. A bass who has had its fill of tasty bluegill may pursue an angler's lure just as aggressively as a hungry bass.

Yet despite their voracious eating habits, largemouths will not take the same lure or bait from day to day. And if the bait or lure is not handled properly, the bass will either ignore it or spit it out just as quickly as it inhaled it. Over the years, bass anglers have developed quite an impressive arsenal of lures, baits, spinners, and spoons, each requiring a specific angling method to be effective. Following is a brief guide to each type of bait and lure with general guidelines on when and how to use them.

PLASTIC WORMS

Virtually any experienced bass angler will tell you that the plastic worm is the most popular and consistently successful of all artificial bass lures. Designed to imitate salamanders, eels, lizards, small snakes, and the venerable nightcrawler, plastic worms are effective in most any season and in a wide variety of angling situations.

The natural feel of a plastic worm makes it one of the most effective lures for largemouth bass. These worms come in a variety of sizes and colors, and can be fished in virtually any situation and during all seasons.

They can be jigged from a boat, crawled along the bottom, fished shallow or deep, or slithered in and around the thickest weed beds. When fished properly, plastic worms have a tantalizingly lifelike action that virtually no hungry bass can resist. And once inhaled by the bass, this supple lure feels like natural food, giving the angler a few extra precious seconds to set the hook.

Plastic worms come in a wide variety of colors and designs, and range in size anywhere from 4 to 12 inches (10 to 30 cm). The most popular colors at the national bass-fishing championships are purple, black, brown, grape, strawberry, yellow, and red. Some worms are speckled with metal flakes or have fluorescent tails—firetails—in an attempt to make them more effective in murky water or on overcast days. Although no color preferences have ever been proven, most experienced anglers believe that translucent worms in soft colors such as blue, red, or strawberry work best in very clear water and solid gaudy colors such as yellow, red, or chartreuse work best in murky or cloudy water. Purple, blue, brown, and black are old standbys that seem to work in almost any type of water.

Water temperature and fish size are the two main considerations when determining what size of worm to use. As a general rule, smaller worms, 4 to 6 inches (10 to 15 cm), are best during cool weather when bass are not feeding as actively; 6- to 9-inch (15- to 20-cm) worms work best in most normal angling situations; and the long 8- to 12-inch (20- to 30-cm) worms are used mostly by professional bassers fishing for trophy-sized fish in heavy cover.

Choose a hook according to the size of the worm—the larger the worm, the larger the hook. Using a large hook on a small worm will ruin the lifelike action of the lure. On the

© Wally Eberhart

other hand, if the hook is too small, it will be next to impossible to set the hook in the tough jaws of a large bass. With a 4-inch (10-cm) worm, use a 1/0 hook; with a 6-inch (15-cm) worm, use a 1/0 to 2/0 hook; with a 7-inch (17-cm) worm, use a 2/0 to 3/0 hook; and with a 9-inch (22-cm) worm, use a 4/0 to 5/0 hook.

When fishing the worm along the bottom, you will need a cone- or bullet-shaped sinker to reach the proper depth. As with almost any type of fishing, use the lightest sinker possible to get your lure where you need it. In most situations, a 1/16- to 1/8-ounce (1.75- to 3.5-g) sinker will be heavy enough in water less than 6 feet (2 m) deep; a 1/8- to 1/4-ounce (3.5- to 7-g) sinker for 6 to 12 feet (2 to 3.6 m); a 1/4- to 3/8-ounce (7- to 10.5-g) sinker for 13 to 18 feet (3.9 to 6 m); and a 3/8- to 1/2-ounce (10.5- to 14-g) sinker for water deeper than 18 feet (6 m). Of course, if you are surface fishing, you will not use a sinker. Some manufacturers make worms

Left: ***An angler heads out to fish for bass on a rainy day.*** **Right:** ***A largemouth explodes through the surface after being hooked with a plastic worm.***

© Wally Eberhart

with extra flotation solely for use on the surface.

Many different rigs have been used with the plastic worm since its invention almost forty years ago; however, none have proven as effective as the basic Texas-style rig. In this rig, the hook is threaded through the tip of the worm and the point is turned back into the head of the worm to make it weedless, meaning the point is not exposed and will not get snagged in the weeds. A weedless lure is essential when going for bass, who love to hide in weed beds, under logs, and around other types of structure. Some hooks have barbs on their shanks to keep the worm from slipping down; however, this can make it difficult to release a well-hooked fish. Another method to prevent slippage is to push the eye of the hook down into the plastic worm, spear a toothpick through both the tip of the worm and the hook eye and trim the ends of the toothpick.

While plastic worms are the most popular bass lures, few anglers have mastered the skill required to fish

© Wally Eberhart

Left: ***When rigged in a "weedless" style, such as the Texas-rig, a plastic worm can be effectively fished in or around dense weedbeds and other types of structure.*** **Right:** ***V-shaped, metallic spinnerbaits attract bass with a combination of action, color, and sound. This combination spinner and jig is probably the second most effective lure for catching largemouths.***

them effectively. Plastic worms demand a delicate touch. A strike may feel like nothing more than a light tap. A bass may inhale the worm with a quick gulp, and if the angler is not ready, it will spit the worm out before the hook can be set. Plastic worms also demand a good sense of timing. The bass may play with the worm before actually taking it. Strike too soon and you will pull the worm away from the fish's mouth. Strike too late and you may hook nothing but water.

To fish a Texas-rigged worm, cast the lure to the spot you believe that bass are holding. Allow the lure to sink, without giving it too much slack; many times bass hit the worm as it is settling to the bottom. Next, slowly retrieve the worm by gently lifting and dropping the rod tip. Keep a tight line as you lower the rod tip, reeling in line—and always, always be ready for a strike. When you detect a pickup, lower the rod tip and point it directly at the bass. As the bass inhales the worm, jerk the rod up hard and fast to set the hook. Bass have extremely tough jaws so a good swift tug is needed to set the hook properly. Once hooked, the bass will immediately dive for cover and try to snap your line. Maintain steady pressure with your rod so the fish cannot wrap the line around a log or boulder.

It takes many hours of trial and error to master the art of fishing with a plastic worm. Those who are good at it develop an uncanny sense of touch and timing and will frequently pull in the biggest largemouths. As with most styles of fishing, however, practice is the key. The more familiar you become with the worm, the more fish you catch.

SPINNERBAITS

That spinnerbaits are the second most effective lure for catching largemouth bass is testament to the fact that largemouths are not finicky eaters. These V-shaped, metallic contraptions do not attempt to imitate any type of natural food. Instead, they attract the bass with a combination of action, color, and sound.

A combination spinner and jig, the

Courtesy Eppinger

basic design of the spinnerbait is a safety-pin-like wire frame with one or two spinners on the top wire, and a vinyl, rubber, or hair skirt around an upward-facing hook on the bottom wire. As the lure is pulled through the water, the blades of the spinners whirl in a flash of metallic color. Spinnerbaits are available in a variety of makeups, sizes, and colors. They are made with large blades, and small, propeller buzzing, single, and tandem blades. Many anglers continually alter and customize their favorite spinners in an endless search for the ultimate bass weapon.

Spinnerbaits are most effective when bass are in shallow water in the spring or fall. Because their hooks are upturned and partially protected by the upper arm of the lure, spinners work very well when fishing in and around the weed beds, fallen trees, rock piles, and other structure that bass frequent. The most basic method for fishing a spinnerbait is to retrieve it about one foot (30 cm) below the surface, so that the lure is still visible. Cast a few feet past the structure you are fishing and reel it in with moderate speed so that you can get the proper action from the spinners.

Buzzing is another popular method of retrieving a spinnerbait. In this method, the bait is quickly retrieved just below the surface of the water, creating a noticeable disturbance. This method is particularly effective for night fishing, when the bass can't necessarily see the lure but will strike at fluttering surface noises. A few manufacturers make

© Hanson Carroll

An angler reaches for a lunker he nabbed with bright yellow crankbait.

"buzz baits," which are specifically designed for this method. A buzz bait is nothing more than a spinnerbait with large propeller-like blades designed to churn up the water.

Flutter fishing is an effective technique for fishing around rock piles, fallen trees, and other underwater obstructions. Cast just past the obstruction you are fishing and let the spinnerbait sink freely to the bottom. As it sinks, the blades of the lure will rotate and attract the attention of the bass. Next, raise the tip of your rod so that the lure darts up along the side of the obstruction and then let it flutter back down. Do not allow too much slack on your line as the spinnerbait is sinking, because this is the time when the bass is most likely to strike.

The best advice for fishing with spinnerbaits is to experiment with many different styles of retrieve. No single method works all of the time. On any given day, you should switch around with your retrieve until you find something that works. Stick with it until it ceases to work, and then go on to another method.

Norman's Deep N, Lazy Ike, Wally Diver, Reel Wee-R, Bagley's Balsa... some of the names of the most popular crankbaits are almost as colorful as the lures themselves.

CRANKBAIT

In the early 1970s, a group of Tennessee anglers developed what is considered the first crankbait—the Big O. Since then, the crankbait has rapidly grown in popularity and can now be found in virtually every bass angler's tackle box. Little more than modified plugs, the original crankbaits float when at rest, but quickly dive to a specified depth when retrieved. Today, crankbaits are divided into three categories: "floating-diving," which, like the originals, float when at rest and dive when retrieved; "minnows," which either float or sink; and "bratting plugs," which only sink.

Floating-diving crankbaits, the most common, have metal or plastic lips that determine how far the lure will sink when retrieved. These colorful lures swim anywhere from a few inches under the surface to 15 feet (5 m) down. If you are fishing any deeper than 15 feet (5 m), you usually have to add a small sinker to a large-lipped crankbait.

Crankbaits can be used all year long and are particularly good for locating bass, because you can cover a lot of water in a short amount of time. The basic method of fishing a crankbait is to simply cast the lure and bring it back using steady, moderate retrieve; however, altering the speed of the retrieve or using a jerky start-and-stop retrieve should be tried until you can determine what method works best. If you are fishing with a few other people, it is good for each of you to use lures that dive to different depths until you determine exactly where the fish are.

© Wally Eberhart

When the fish are holding deep and around a large structure, the jig may be your best lure choice. While the technique for jigging is relatively simple, it does require a keen sense of feel and timing.

© Wally Eberhart

Floating crankbaits have small lips that make the lure wobble when retrieved. These lures should be fished in the same way as surface lures (see page 40). Sinking crankbaits should be fished using a counting system. Cast the lure and then begin counting as it sinks. Begin your retrieve at different counts until you determine at what depth the fish are feeding.

Made of molded plastic, metal, or wood, crankbaits can be anywhere from 3 to 9 inches (8 to 22 cm) long, however, the most versatile sizes are 3 and 4 inches (8 and 10 cm). Some manufacturers add rattle chambers filled with tiny ball bearings to these lures to create extra noise and action. The most popular crankbaits for bass include: Norman's Deep N, Natural Ike, Cotton Cordell Wally Diver, Lazy Ike, Rebel Wee-R, Mann's Deep Pig, and Bagley's Balsa B.

Jigging Lures

When all else fails, a jigging lure may be your best bet for drawing at least a few strikes. The most common jig is a *leadhead jig*. This consists of a weighed lure made of metal (usually lead) with a nylon skirt, hair, plastic attractor, feather, or bucktail attached. Some anglers tip their jigs with live bait to make them a little more enticing.

Jigging is similar to worm fishing in that the technique itself seems simple; however, it requires a keen sense of feel and timing on the part of the angler. It requires a vertical style of fishing, where you raise and lower the rod lip so that the jig rises and falls in sudden, flashy movements. Bass usually hit the line when the lure is falling, with a gentle, almost unnoticeable strike.

Jigging is particularly effective when the fish are holding deep around large structures such as rock piles, boulders, bridge pilings, and sunken trees. Other types of available jigging lures include: jigging spoons, vibrating blades, and tailspins. Additionally, the most popular bass jigs include: Ugly Bug, Metal Flake Flippin' Jig, and Uncle Buck's Crappie Bug.

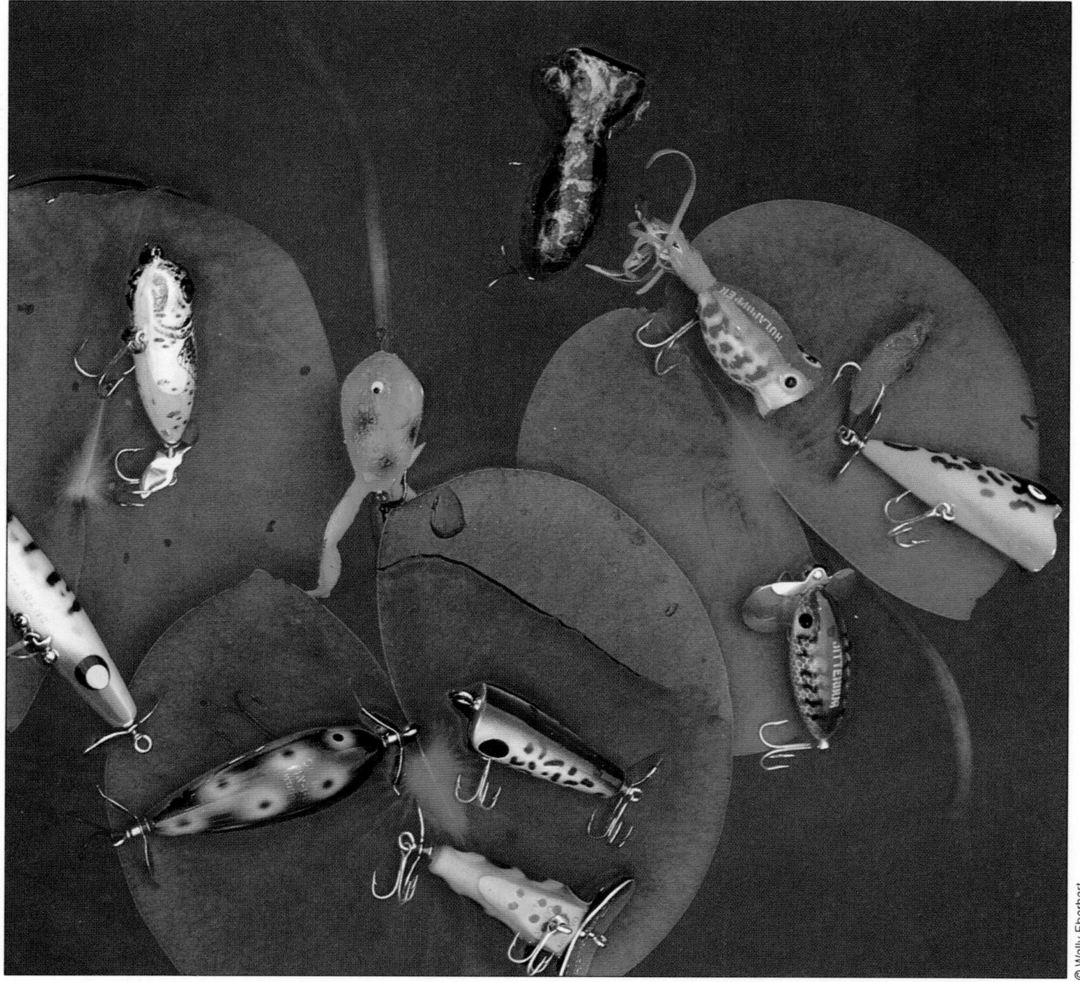

© Wally Eberhart

Surface lures come in four basic types: swimming plugs, poppers, chuggers, and stickbaits. Each is designed to attract the lure through a combination of movement and sound.

SURFACE LURES

One of the most exhilarating sights in all of bass fishing is a hungry bass charging to the surface to hit a plug. In a sudden flash of blue, the fish breaks the surface, inhales the plug, and, once hooked, puts up a hearty, desperate fight.

Surface lures work best in calm, warm water when the bass are feeding in shallow areas. They are also a very good choice for night fishing, because bass rely more on sound and vibration for finding food when visibility is low. If the water is at all choppy, however, or below 60°F (16°C), surface lures may be ineffective.

There are four basic types of surface lures used in bass fishing: swimming plugs, poppers, chuggers, and stickbaits.

Swimming plugs

Swimming plugs are designed to imitate small fish or other amphibious life, such as frogs, salamanders, or eels. When retrieved, these lures suggest the swimming motion of the quarry they imitate. While they are usually fished just below the surface, they can also be skittered across the top, creating a noisy wake. A few popular swimming plugs are Lazy Ike, Rapala, Les Davis Witch Doctor, Creek Chub Pikie, and Flatfish.

Poppers

These lures are specifically designed as surface-disturbing plugs. When retrieved they create a gurgling, bubbling, and popping sound on the water's surface. Poppers should be retrieved in a series of starts and stops. Cast the lure out and let it rest for a few minutes. Then retrieve it a few feet and let it rest again. The popping and gurgling will gain the fish's attention. Bass usually follow a popper for several starts and stops before striking. The strikes usually come when the lure is at rest. Classic poppers include the Hula-Popper and the Gaines Spin Popper.

Chuggers

Chuggers are little more than high-tech poppers. In addition to the classic bubbling and gurgling of a normal popper, chuggers churn the water with specially fitted blades,

Surface lures work best in calm, warm water when the bass are feeding in shallow areas. Here an angler used a surface lure to nab a bass from a lily pond.

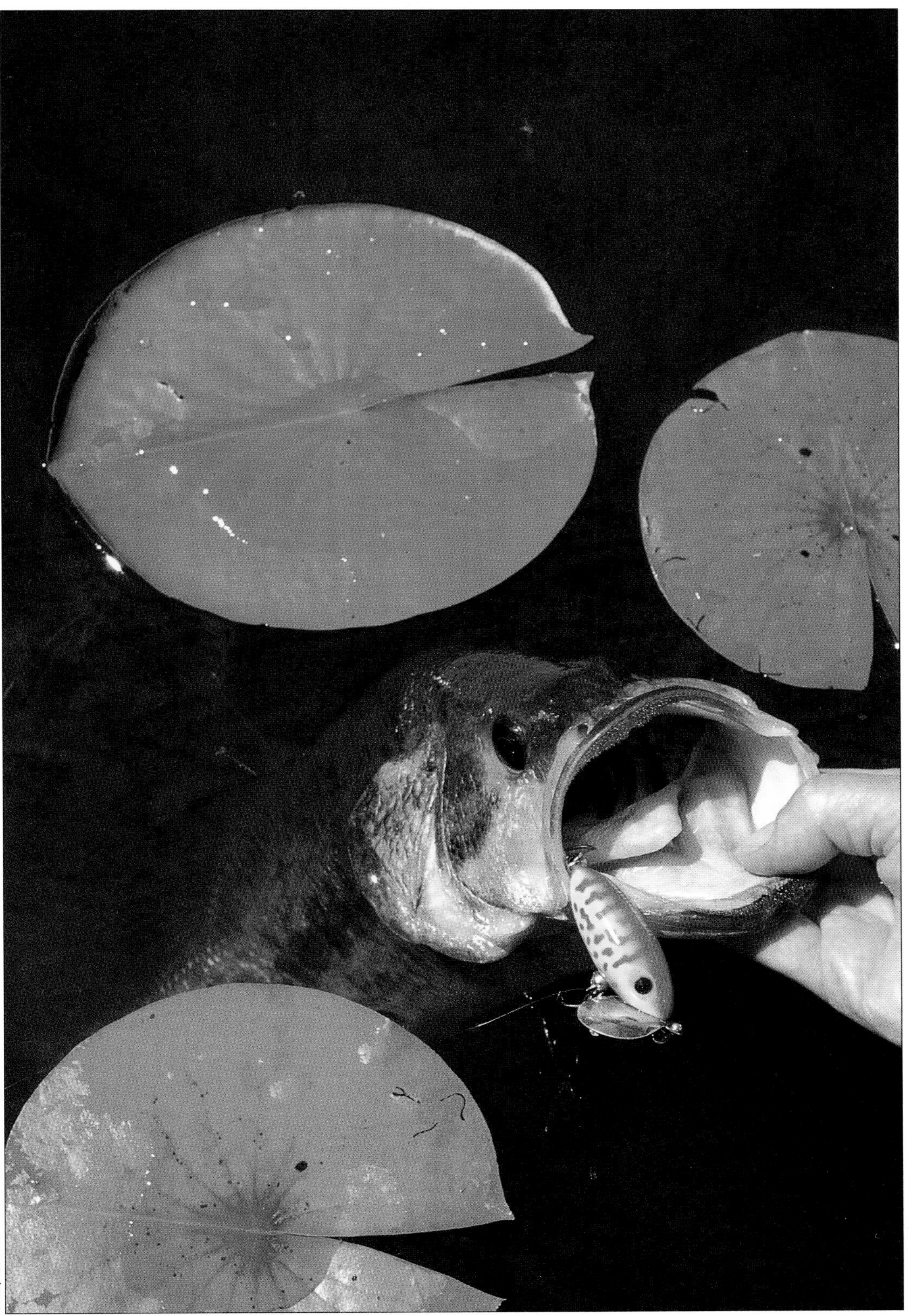

© Wally Eberhart

propellers, or an extra nose fin. These noisy lures are especially good for night fishing. The most famous of all chuggers is the Arbogast Jitterbug. Developed in the early 1930s, this classic lure imitates the movements of a wounded bait fish or frog.

Buzz baits

These lures resemble spinnerbaits in basic design (see page 34), however, here the blade revolves around a shaft rather than spinning on a swivel. In addition, buzz baits usually have large aluminum propellers instead of the standard spinner, making them ideal surface-disturbing lures.

Stickbaits

The least complex of the surface-disturbing plugs, stickbaits offer no action on their own. When retrieved steadily across the surface, they create little disturbance. The angler must impart action on the stickbait with swift tugs and jerks on the line. The trick in fishing this type of lure is creating the natural-looking yet erratic action of an injured bait fish.

© Wally Eberhart

Courtesy Luhr-Jensen (both)

Spoons are extremely simple, yet effective lures. These bent, metal blades wobble back and forth when retrieved, imitating the action of a minnow. Still, live bait, such as this leopard frog, is most effective for catching large, trophy-sized bass.

SPOONS

Spoons are the most basic of all artificial lures. Nothing more than a bent metal blade with a hook, the spoon simply wobbles back and forth like a minnow when retrieved. While spoons come in both standard and weedless designs, the weedless is the best choice for fishing the heavy structure that bass love. They can be worked in and around thick weed beds and lily pads effectively without getting snagged. Many anglers add a small twister tail or a strip of pork rind to add a little extra action to their spoons. The most popular spoons on the market are the Johnson Silver Minnow, Eppinger Daredevle, and Cather's Spoons.

LIVE BAIT

While the vast majority of bass anglers use artificial lures, there are many situations where live bait is much more effective. If bass are sluggish because of adverse water conditions, in most cases they will only go after slow-moving quarry, and most lures lose their enticing action when worked slowly. Also, in clear, cool water, bass examine their food much more closely and either ignore or immediately spit out anything that does not look or feel natural.

The effectiveness of live bait for snagging trophy-size bass is well documented. Both the second largest (21 pounds, 3 ounces [9 kg, 84 g]) and the third largest (20 pounds, 15 ounces [9 kg, 420 g]) bass on record were caught using live bait. Extremely large old bass are much more careful about what they eat than are younger, more carefree bass. So, although you may catch more bass with a lure, you will most likely catch larger bass with live bait.

As stated earlier, largemouth bass are very undiscerning eaters. They feed on a wider variety of prey than any other freshwater game fish; therefore the bass angler has a lot of leeway in choosing bait. The most popular baits are frogs, crawfish, minnows, nightcrawlers, and salamanders. Frogs have long been considered the best live bait for largemouths, however, in recent years natural frog populations have drastically dropped because of pollution and disease. When fishing with a live frog—or any type of live bait, for that matter—always use a weedless hook. Once cast, the frog will immediately swim for weeds, lily pads, or other types of cover. The weedless hook keeps your line from snagging.

The best way of hooking frogs, minnows, and salamanders is through the lips. This way the bait will stay lively cast after cast, and will still swim freely and naturally. Choose a hook according to the size of the bait. If the hook is too small, the bass will steal your bait. If the hook is too large, the bait won't look natural.

© Wally Eberhart

While artificial lures are the most popular devices for catching largemouths, in many situations, nothing is more effective than natural bait. This is especially true when going after large, trophy-sized bass, who are more particular about what they eat.

Crawfish, the most popular bait for smallmouth bass, also work well for largemouths. Crawfish should be hooked through the tail and crawled slowly along the bottom. When using nightcrawlers, the angler has a couple different rigging options. One is the same Texas rig used for fishing plastic worms. For really large bass, however, a wiggling glob of worms is much better.

As with plastic worms, natural bait should be fished using the lightest sinker possible to reach the required depth. Also, cone or bullet sinkers will result in fewer snags and a more natural movement when fishing heavy structure.

Your choice of bait or lure depends greatly on the conditions you are fishing. The primary concern is the depth that the fish are feeding. In water under ten feet (3 m) deep, use surface lures, spinnerbaits, spinners, shallow crankbaits, or plastic worms. In deeper water, jigging lures, deep-running crankbaits, and heavily weighted plastic worms work best. Live bait seems to work well in almost any situation. As you clock more and more bass-fishing hours you will acquire a knack for choosing the right bait or lure for the right situation. The best advice is to examine the fishing conditions, to ask for guidance from anglers familiar with the waters you are fishing, and, finally, to try many different lures and bass-fishing methods until you discover what works most effectively.

© Wally Eberhart

Chapter 3

ANGLING NOTES

Not too long ago largemouth bass were only found east of the Mississippi and south of the Great Lakes. However, rigorous and highly successful stocking programs over the past forty years or so have brought this hardy gamefish to virtually every state in the continental United States, as well as southern Canada and most of Mexico. As the number of largemouths across North America grew, so did the fish's popularity among freshwater anglers. The largemouth is a very smart and unpredictable fish. It is an expert at hiding in thick weed beds and under jagged overhangs. In addition, the largemouth seldom travels too far in search of food, so the angler must take the lure or bait to the fish in order to be successful. All these characteristics make largemouth fishing an exciting sport.

EQUIPMENT FOR THE LARGEMOUTH

When angling for the largemouth bass, it is very important to have the proper equipment. While a few anglers do fish for largemouths with spinning or fly outfits, the vast majority of successful bass busters use a bait-casting outfit. A 5- to 7-foot (1.5- to 2-m) bait-casting rod matched with a lightweight bait-casting reel fitted with 8- to 10-pound- (4- to 4.5-kg-) test provides the angler with just the right combination of casting accuracy and fish-fighting power.

Courtesy Cabela's

Right: *A happy angler displays a healthy-sized bass he caught with his medium-weight bait-casting rod. Bait-casting equipment is the outfit of choice among serious bass anglers.*

Bait-casting has recently been revived. After World War II, many anglers put their old bait casters in the closet in favor of the new, easy-to-use spinning outfits. Over the past twenty-five years, however, bait-casting technology has been improved upon to such an extent that, today, most serious bass anglers have made bait-casting equipment their outfit of choice.

In the old days, when the reels were cast, the spool, gears, and handle all revolved simultaneously, making it difficult for the angler to control. If thumb pressure wasn't applied at just the right time to drop the lure in the water, a serious backlash would occur, causing the line to tangle up in what became known as a bird's nest. In addition, when a big fish hit the line on an old bait caster, the spool and handle would both start spinning furiously, often jamming the angler's thumb or scraping his/her knuckles.

Today, most high-quality bait casters are built with magnetic anti-backlash technology and a level-wind mechanism (a guide that evenly places retrieved line on the spool). However, the most significant development in bait-casting equipment is free-spool casting. This means that only the spool rotates during the cast, making it much easier to control the flow of the line and to avoid backlash.

Bait-casting outfits are divided into three categories: lightweights, medium-weights, and heavyweights. *Lightweight* rods run from 5 to 6½ feet (1 to 2.5 cm) in length and have a very limber action. Designed primarily for crappie fishing, these outfits can accurately cast lures and baits weighing between ⅛- and ¼-ounce (3.5- and 7-g)—lures wrongly considered by many as being light for bass fishing. Lightweight rods, however, may lack the backbone necessary to pull in the big lunkers.

Courtesy Cabela's

A variety of spinning and bait-casting rods are displayed on a handsome display rack. Advances in technology over the past several years have made bait-casting rods much easier to use. As a result, many anglers are returning to bait-casting equipment for bass fishing.

Medium-weight rods are often a bit shorter than lightweights (between $4\frac{1}{2}$ and 6 feet (1.5 and 2 m), however, they are much stiffer, have reinforced butts, less taper, and can cast slightly bigger lures and baits (between $\frac{3}{8}$ and $\frac{3}{4}$ of an ounce [10.5 and 21 g]). These outfits are designed to be worked in small, overgrown creeks and rivers where accurate casting is a must. They are the best overall choice for stream-bound smallmouth bass and fishing for small largemouths.

Heavyweight baitcasting rods are about the same length as lightweight rods, but much stiffer and more powerful. These stable rods can easily handle lures and baits as heavy as $1\frac{1}{2}$ to 2 ounces (42 to 56 g) and can throw line testing between 15 to 20 pounds (7 to 10 kg). Most freshwater angling, however, does not require line any heavier than 15-pound (7-kg) test. These are the most popular outfits for snagging big largemouths and smallmouths, as well as pike and muskies, but are on the heavy side for everyday angling.

Even with all of the improvements over the past twenty-five years, the

Look for largemouth bass in and around underwater brush, next to trees, in weedbeds, and in the shade from undercut banks.

bait caster is still a fairly tricky outfit to handle. While backlash has been cut down, it has not been totally eliminated. The angler must have a lot of practice and good timing to effectively cast with this outfit. In the right hands, the bait caster can be a deadly accurate tool.

LOCATING THE FISH

Of course, even if you have all the latest gear—a finely tuned bait-casting reel, a high-powered bass boat laden with electronics, a tackle box full of the most popular spoons, spinners, plugs, and chuggers—you still won't catch any bass if you don't know where they are. Finding the fish is often the most difficult part of bass fishing. Bass are very tenacious fish, and they love to hide in a variety of natural hiding places.

Largemouths also move about a lake, pond, reservoir, or stream as the seasons and water conditions change. Time of year, water temperatures, water levels, weather, light, and the availability of food are all contributing factors to the migrating characteristics of the largemouth bass.

Early spring is one of the easiest times to catch largemouth bass. As the water warms up after the winter chill, the fish become more active and begin feeding heavily in preparation for their spring spawning season. They hold close to shore and near the surface, feeding on ample supplies of spring baitfish. After spawning actually begins, they feed little but they will attack any trespasser in their spawning grounds. In Florida and other southern states, spawning may begin as early as January, February,

© W.A. Banaszewski/Visuals Unlimited

Left: ***An ice fisherman pulls a largemouth from the deep. While it is possible to catch largemouths in the dead of winter, it can be very difficult. Most of the fish will remain in deep water in a state of near hibernation.*** **Right:** ***A young boy does some jigging off of a pier on a summer evening. In the summer, bass usually move into deeper, cooler, and more oxygenated waters.***

or March. In northern climates, however, spawning usually won't occur until April or June.

As summer sets in and the water continues to warm up, bass retreat to deeper, cooler, more oxygenated waters. Just how deep they go depends on particular factors of each lake or reservoir—current, structure, temperature, oxygen, and availability of food. The larger fish tend to go into deeper waters, while the smaller fish may stay in relatively shallow areas. Even in the heat of midsummer, however, bass often return to shallow waters to feed in the early morning, evening, and late night hours. Even so, they are rarely found in shallow waters in the middle of the day, especially when the sun is bright and wind is calm.

As the fall sets in and the water begins to cool, largemouths again head for shallow waters. In many areas, bass fishing in the fall is as good as it gets. The fish feed voraciously in preparation for winter and they readily rise to hit a surface lure or plug. In addition, there tend to be a lot fewer anglers on the water

© Bob Firth/Firth PhotoBank

in fall, which means more solitude and less competition.

In northern regions, winter fishing for bass is virtually nonexistent. The fish hold in deep water in a state of near hibernation. In the Deep South, however, where water temperatures never go too low, fishing can be good throughout the winter. The fish are in deep water, but they remain fairly active. Trolling and deep jigging are about the only ways to pull them out in the winter.

No matter what the season, it is important to be familiar with the

© Bob Firth/Firth Photobank

When fishing in unfamiliar waters, it is a good idea to hire a guide, or at least buy a topographical map of the area. By studying a map, you can locate the different types of structure that will most likely attract largemouths.

contours, depths, and structure characteristics of the lake, river, or reservoir you are fishing. If you are fishing a lake for the first time, it is a good idea to hire a guide or to go out with an angler who is familiar with the water, somone who knows the hot spots and the bottom geography. A knowledgeable angler can save you hours of hit-or-miss fishing. Blind fishing for bass is almost always a waste of time.

If you are on your own, talk to local marina operators, tackle shop owners, and other anglers to find out where the most productive areas are. Another good piece of advice is to simply watch other anglers on the lake. Find out where they go at various times of day and what type of tackle they use. You can learn almost as much by studying other anglers as you can by studying the lake itself.

All tackle shops and marinas sell topographical and hydrographic maps of local waters. Buy a few of these maps and study them carefully. Make note of where the lake's contours, points, drop-offs, and depth changes are located, remembering that bass love structure and unusual terrain. These maps are indispensable aids in locating largemouths. Experienced bass busters can take a quick look at a map and determine in which areas the fish are most likely to be—even if they have never fished that lake before. In addition to maps, a reliable depthfinder is essential equipment for bass fishing. This electronic device will help to easily locate structure, unusual contours, and schools of bait fish—all indications that bass may be nearby.

Largemouths are easiest to locate and catch when they are feeding on or near the surface in shallow water. As stated earlier, this usually occurs in the spring or fall, or around dawn, dusk, and during the night in the

© Bob Firth/Firth Photobank

summer. Look for them near some sort of cover. They will hold under lily pads, overhanging trees, undercut banks, brush, or in the middle of dense weed beds or reed patches. In rivers, largemouths tend to avoid the stronger currents in favor of the calmer eddies, pools, and coves. Largemouths love to forage for bait fish where small streams empty into a river or lake. If the fish are not hitting in these areas, look for them around points that slope into deep water, along shallow-water ridges and ledges, or around rock piles or sunken trees.

SPRING ANGLING NOTES

As stated earlier, spring bass fishing can be some of the best fishing of the year. This is particularly true just before the spawning season, when the fish are very active and hungry and will strike at virtually anything that moves. Many anglers, however, do not approve of fishing for bass prior to the spawning season, even where it is legal. They feel the fish are too easy to catch at this vulnerable time and that overfishing can do

Dense lily and weed beds, such as the one below, are favorite hiding places of big largemouths. Here an angler pulls a lunker from the lily pads.

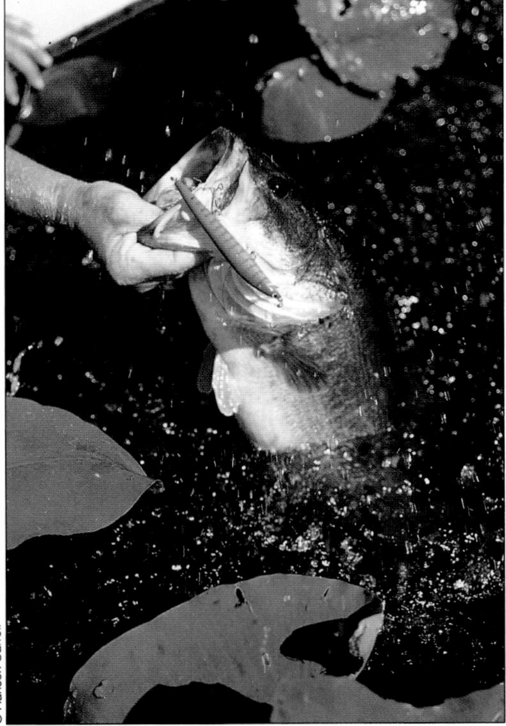

© Hanson Carroll

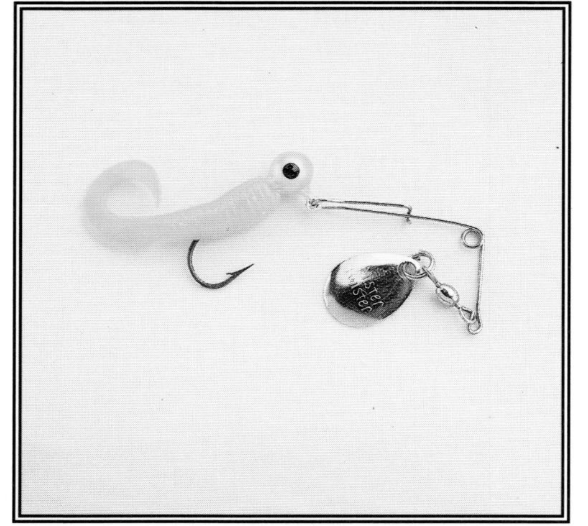

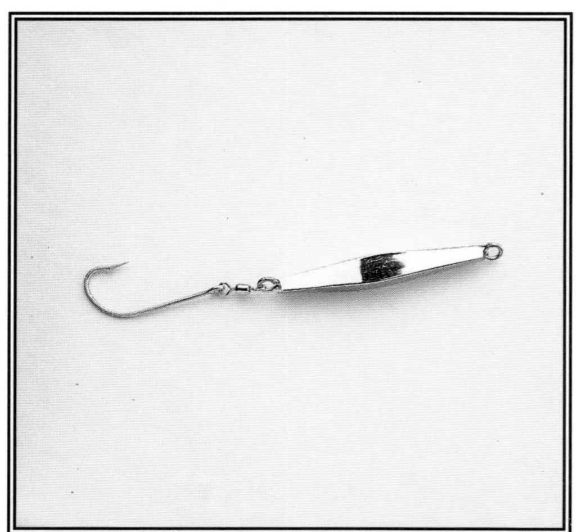

Largemouth bass will go after a variety of spinnerbaits, jigs, plugs, and poppers such as, **clockwise from upper left,** ***Mr. Twister, Diamond Jig, Hopkins NO-EQL, and Cisco Kid Salty Super Husky, as well as,*** **opposite page,** ***the Luhr-Jensen J-Plug.***

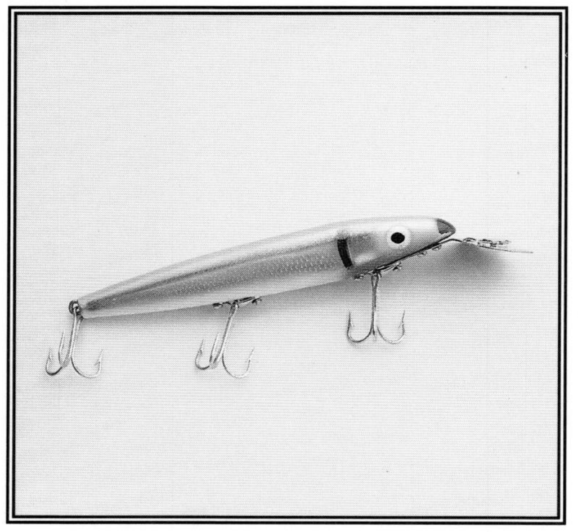

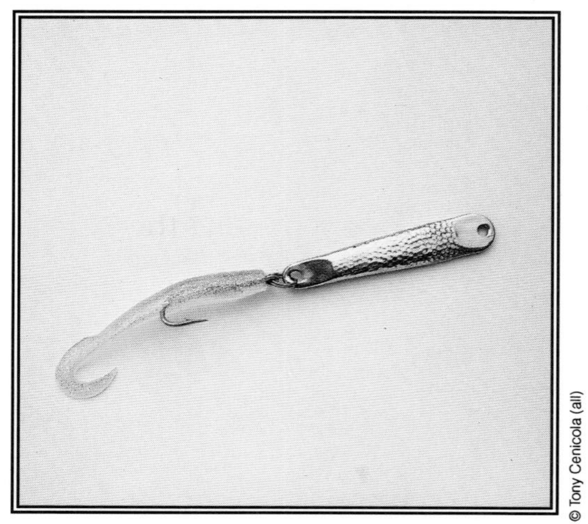

© Tony Cenicola (all)

irreparable harm to the bass populations. In fact, many areas do not allow any bass fishing until the local spawning season is over. If you decide to fish in early spring you should practice catch and release fishing. Gently release all the fish you catch before spawning is completed. This will help ensure a healthy new population of fry, and better bass fishing in the future.

Even after the spawning season, largemouths will remain in shallow waters anywhere from several weeks to a few months. The temperature of the water will help determine just how actively the fish are feeding. If temperatures are too cold, they will hold on the bottom and wait for their quarry to come to them. In these conditions it is necessary to take the bait or lure directly to the fish. They will most likely be located on the shallow side of a sharp drop-off or along the edges of a jutting point. Rig your outfit with a spinnerbait or a jig and cast directly to where the fish are holding. Let the lure flutter to the bottom and then retrieve it with short quick jerks, occasionally lifting the lure from the bottom and letting it gently flutter back to the bottom. Largemouths generally hit the lure as it is sinking directly in front of their nose.

Largemouths feed most actively in the spring when water temperatures are between 55°and 60°F (13°and 16°C). They will cruise through extremely shallow waters in search of crawfish, minnows, and other small quarry. A Texas-rigged plastic worm is probably the best overall lure for shallow-water bass fishing. If possible, fish parallel to the shore, either crawling the worm along the bottom or retrieving it with a constant lifting and sinking motion.

Spinnerbaits can also be quite effective for nabbing bass in extremely shallow water. One method is to actually cast the lure directly onto the shore and then drag it off into the water. This method is particularly effective when the bass are hugging the shore in search of food.

The most exciting bass fishing comes when the fish are actively feeding on the surface. When this occurs, a shallow-diving crankbait or other surface plug can trigger explosive, water-churning strikes. Once hooked, the bass will probably head for deep water and attempt to free itself by snagging your line on some sort of obstruction. Play your fish carefully and try to keep it from heading into dense structure. Do not, however, attempt to reel it in too quickly. Largemouths are extremely strong fish and may still have some fight left in them even after several long runs.

SUMMER ANGLING NOTES

Experienced bass anglers do most of their serious fishing in the summer, when the lake or reservoir's ecosystem is in full swing. With their spawning responsibilities behind them, largemouths are able to concentrate on what they do best—eat. And in the summer, there is plenty of food for the largemouth to prey on. The lakes and reservoirs will be brimming with insects, salamanders, frogs, newly hatched fry, crawfish, and other largemouth delicacies.

The real art in bass fishing is in being able to yank the fish out of dense, heavy structure. The Texas-rigged plastic worm is the most effective lure for landing big lunkers in the summer as well as the spring. Because the hook point is stuck back into the worm in this weedless-style rig, the angler can crawl the plastic worm through the thickest of weed beds without snagging the lure. Weedless spoons are also very effective for fishing heavy structure. While these lures do not really resemble any type of natural prey, their action alone, as they crawl and flutter through weed beds, is enough to entice many bass into striking.

There is no hard and fast rule as to how a bass will take your lure. It may strike hard and fast, instantly bending your rod as it heads for deep water. On the other hand, many times a bass will inhale your lure, realize it's artificial, and spit it back out without your even noticing a twinge on your line. This is one of the reasons why plastic worms are such effective lures. They feel natural in the bass's mouth, giving you a few extra precious seconds to notice the strike and set the hook. Always be alert for tugs and yanks on your line. As you gain more fishing experience

Courtesy Luhr-Jensen

In the fall, largemouths will again move back into shallow water. At this time, top water lures, such as those used in the spring, can be very effective.

© Wally Eberhart

you will be able to tell the difference between the vibrations caused by the lure going over heavy structure and the sometimes gentle tug of a striking bass.

With summer bass fishing, it is extremely important to know your fishing hole well. Take time to scrutinize the area. A good pair of polarized sunglasses will cut the surface glare and help you to see directly to the bottom of the lake. Examine the weed beds for holes, dips, bends, and open pockets. Pay close attention to where the shadows fall and how they shift as the sun moves across the sky, remembering that bass are sensitive to bright light. Also, study the behavior of the bass themselves. Look for their strongholds and take note of their feeding characteristics. What type of quarry are they feeding on? Are they actively pursuing their prey, or are they waiting for the food to come to them? Are they striking quickly? Or, are they, like you, studying their prey before attacking? The better you know the fish and their habitat, the better your chances will be of landing a prize-winning bass.

FALL ANGLING NOTES

When the water begins to cool off again in the fall, largemouths move back into shallow water and again feed close to the surface. In many areas, fishing remains good until as late as November or early December. Because the bass are again feeding in shallow water, anglers can use many of the same angling techniques in the fall that they use in the spring.

Topwater lures such as shallow-diving crankbaits, chuggers, poppers, swimming plugs, and buzz baits can lead to very exciting fishing any time largemouths are hitting on

© John Gerlach/Visuals Unlimited

While most winter bass fishing is done in the Deep South, where the fish remain active year-round, a few hearty souls in the North cut a hole in the ice to fish for the lethargic winter bass.

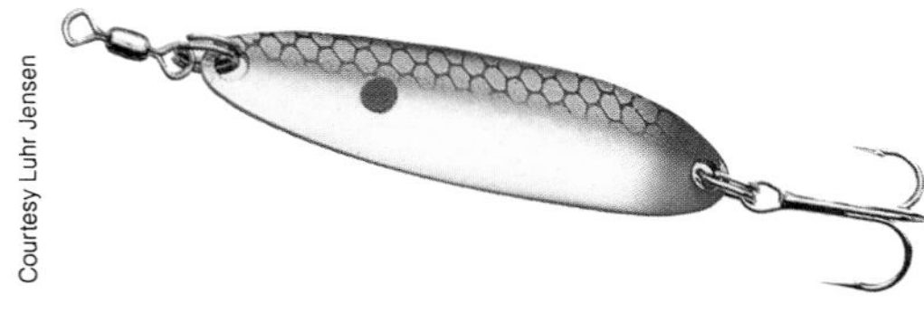

Courtesy Luhr Jensen

or near the surface. Crankbaits are especially good for locating bass, because they enable the angler to cover a lot of water in a short amount of time. Simply cast the lure and let it rest on the surface of the water for a few seconds. Then begin to reel it in using a steady, moderate retrieve. As you begin the retrieve, the lure will dive under the surface of the water. By varying your reeling speed, you can cause the lure to dive down deeper or rise toward the surface.

In general, surface lures work best in calm, warm water and at night, when the bass rely more on sound and vibration for finding food. If the water is choppy, however, or below 60°F (16°C), surface lures may be ineffective, so always take note of water conditions when fishing in the fall.

WINTER ANGLING NOTES

In most parts of North America, winter bass fishing is spotty at best. A few northern ice anglers take an occasional bass, but for the most part winter fishing is limited to the more southerly parts of the bass's range. The main problem with winter bass fishing is that once the water drops below 50°F (13°C), the fish become inactive and lethargic, and they feed very little. In addition, they head for deep water and can be very difficult to locate. Once you do locate a bass, however, chances are good that there will be quite a few others in the area. When the water turns cold bass tend to gather together in tight schools.

In cold weather, bass will congregate around deep shorelines, submerged cliffs, and points bordering deep water. As at other times of the year, they will also hold near some sort of structure. Jigging with a spoon is by far the most effective method for pulling bass out of deep cold water. When the first cold weather hits, shad and other baitfish die off in large numbers and sink to the bottom. This is the primary diet of winter largemouths. The action of a jigged spoon closely imitates the fluttering and twitching of dying baitfish. Experiment by jigging at different depths with different types of action on the lure. Once you get a few hits, mark that depth with a piece of tape on your line and fish that depth continually as long as you get strikes. Because bass are inactive in the winter, you should work your jig with a slow, easy motion. In addition, most bass wil hit the lure as it is sinking. Sometimes this strike can be almost imperceivable—just a brief hesitation in the sinking, or a slight tug. Be alert for even the slightest irregularity on your line and set the hook immediately.

The Deep South offers the best winter bass fishing in North America. In the reservoirs of Florida, Mississippi, and Texas, the water never gets too cold and the bass remain fairly active year-round.

Chapter 4

Smallmouth Bass

On the morning of July 9, 1955, D.L. Hayes was trolling for bass around a shale point in Dale Hollow Lake, Kentucky. After a few hours of moderate success, he attached a pearly Bomber to his line in the hope of

© Gregory K. Scott/Nature Photos

improving his luck. At about 10:00 a.m., a huge fish slammed Hayes's line and began a battle that lasted for nearly half an hour. The fish darted for the surface, jumped, tried to shake the line, and then dove for deep water, where it put up a relentless fight. Finally, after what must have seemed like an eternity of rod-bending work, Hayes landed the fish—a world record 27-inch, 11-pound, 15-ounce (67-cm, 5-kg, 420-g) smallmouth bass.

Pound for pound, inch for inch, the smallmouth bass is among the fiercest fighting game fish in North America. It is a very acrobatic fish that strikes hard and runs fast. In addition, the smallmouth is wary and temperamental, making it a challenging fish to fool. Although not as big as its cousin, the largemouth bass, the smallmouth is often preferred by anglers who have fished for both. Unfortunately, the sheer numbers and distribution of the smallmouth are somewhat lim-

The smallmouth bass is a very acrobatic fish that is very hard to fool. Unlike its cousin, the largemouth, the smallmouth bass is very wary and somewhat particular about what it eats.

© Francis & Donna Caldwell

ited, keeping its popularity relatively low among the average angling population.

The smallmouth's natural range runs from southwest Quebec and southeast Ontario, south to Alabama, Georgia, northern Mississippi, and Arkansas. Originally, there were no smallmouth bass found east of the Appalachians or west of eastern Oklahoma. Today, the smallmouth is widely stocked and can be found in varying numbers across southern Canada and in every state except Florida, Louisiana, and Alaska.

The smallmouth bass enjoys the cool, clear waters of the mid-northern states and southern Canada. The finest areas for smallmouths include: Lake Michigan; Les Cheneaux Islands in Lake Huron; the northern Mississippi and Lac La Croix in Minnesota, the Ozark Mountain region in Missouri, the Maumee, Little Darby, and Whetstone rivers in Ohio; the Allegheny Reservoir, Lake Erie, and the Susquehanna and Delaware rivers in Pennsylvania; the St. Lawrence, Niagara, and Delaware rivers in New York; and the Third Machias Lake, Big Lake,

A couple of anglers fish for smallmouth bass and trout on the Madison River in Yellowstone.

Crawford Lake, Pocomoonshine Lake, and the Penobscot and Kennebec rivers in Maine.

Many southern waters are comprised of muddy, weedy lakes and ponds that are more suitable for largemouth than for smallmouth bass. Even in southern areas where smallmouths are present, their numbers are quite small. Smallmouth bass love clear clean waters and usually prefer rivers and streams over lakes and reservoirs. They are seldom found in stagnant ponds or murky lakes shallower than 25 feet (8 cm). Smallmouths tolerate water that is murky for short periods of time, but do not stay in waters where the visibility is less than 1 foot (.3 m) through most of the year.

In addition to clear waters, the smallmouth bass loves to hold in a moderately swift current. In rivers and streams they stay away from the swiftest sections, where the trout might hold, but prefer pools with a noticeable current to those that are completely stagnant. Like their cousins, smallmouths like heavy structure, such as boulders, rock beds, tree

The smallmouth bass can be distinguished by its dark bars, bands, and splotches on its sides. These markings are especially pronounced in males at spawning time.

trunks, and bridge abutments, but stay away from the heavy weed beds that largemouths love so much.

In lakes and reservoirs, smallmouths tend to congregate around the mouths of tributary rivers and streams, or in windy areas where the current is strong. They can also be found holding in shallow areas adjacent to a steep drop-off. In lakes where both large- and smallmouths are present, the smallmouths tend to stay in slightly deeper waters.

The smallmouth bass, or *Micropterus dolomieui*, is also known as the bronzeback, black bass, brown bass, swago bass, green trout, tiger bass, gold bass, and bronze bass. Along with its close relatives, the largemouth and the spotted bass, the smallmouth is designated as a black bass and a member of the sunfish family. Biologists have recently developed a largemouth/smallmouth hybrid, affectionately known as the meanmouth because of its aggressive disposition. While this hybrid may someday pose a new challenge to North American anglers, it is still very much in the experimental stage.

The color of the smallmouth bass varies depending on the water it is in—from pale yellow to dark brown. As a general rule, the clearer the water, the lighter the fish, the more murky the water, the darker the fish. The smallmouth usually has a dark olive back, greenish yellow sides with a bronze luster, and a creamy white belly. The smallmouth also has distinct dark bars, bands, and splotches on its sides. These markings are very pronounced in males at spawning time, giving them an almost tiger-striped appearance.

Mouth size distinctly separates the smallmouth bass from the largemouth. The upper jaw of the small-

© Ron Pittard/Windsor Publications, Inc.

mouth reaches only to the middle of the eye, whereas the jaw of the largemouth extends beyond the rear of the eye. In addition, the smallmouth is slightly smaller and more compressed than the largemouth. In rivers and streams, smallmouth bass average from about ½ to 3 pounds (.3 to 1.3 kg). In the lakes and reservoirs of the southern U.S., where food is abundant and the growing season is longer, the fish tend to grow faster, but they do not live as long. In the northern part of its range, a smallmouth may live as long as eighteen years, whereas seven years is the average life expectancy of a southern smallmouth. No matter where you are fishing, however, a 5- or 6-pounder (2.3- or 2.8-kg) is a good-size fish. Unlike other varieties of fish, both the male and the female smallmouth grow at about the same rate and live to about the same age.

The smallmouth spawns a bit earlier in the spring than other members of the sunfish family in the same area. The exact time of year spawning occurs depends on climate and water temperature. In the far southern regions of the fish's range, smallmouths may spawn as early as March, and in the northern regions as late as May. At the beginning of the spawning cycle, the male chooses a site near an object, such as a rock or log, which protects the nest from strong currents. Most bass spawn in 2 to 5 feet (.6 to 1.5 m) of water; although some nests have been found in water as deep as 20 feet (6 m). In addition, smallmouth bass tend to avoid muddy bottoms as they prefer sandy, gravelly, or rocky bottoms.

As the water temperature hits 55°F (13°C) the male begins digging out a circular nest with wide sweeps

© Gregory K. Scott/Nature Photos

A pensive smallmouth rests on the bottom of a stream, waiting for an unsuspecting baitfish to happen by.

of his tail. Most smallmouth nests have a diameter of about twice the fish's length and are about 2 to 4 inches (5 to 10 cm) deep. Male smallmouths may return year after year to the same nest for spawning. They always build a new nest in the general vicinity of their old nest.

A few days later the females swim into the spawning area. At this time each male makes mad dashes around the area in hopes of impressing a female and coaxing her into his nest. No spawning takes place, however, until the water temperature reaches between 56° and 60° F (13° and 16°C) (a few degrees cooler than with the largemouth). Once the fish are paired off, each couple lie side by side in the nest. Soon the female tilts gently on her side and deposits up to 7,000 eggs per pound of body weight, as the male simultaneously releases his milt.

After spawning, the female swims out to deep water to recuperate, and the male stays behind to guard the nest. Incubation takes anywhere from two to ten days depending on the water temperature. If the temper-

© Wally Eberhart

Crawfish are one of the favorite foods of the smallmouth bass. In certain areas they make up as much as three-quarters of the smallmouth's diet.

Courtesy Orvis Company, Inc.

ature dips below 50°F (10°C), the male may abandon the nest and virtually no offspring will hatch. Even under optimal conditions only about 35 percent of the eggs hatch.

The fry remain in the nest for another week under the watchful eye of the male smallmouth. Even after they leave the nest as fingerlings, the adult male stays in the vicinity for another five days to ward off hungry predators. Despite the efforts of the father, only about 10 percent of all smallmouth fry survive to reach the fingerling stage.

Unlike the largemouths, smallmouth bass are poor competitors. They fall easy prey to larger fish and are unable to compete for food with the other freshwater denizens. If there are an abundance of predator fish, such as northern pike or largemouth bass in the area, most smallmouths will be driven to deeper waters, eaten by larger fish, or starved out of existence.

The crawfish is the favorite food of the smallmouth bass. In areas where crawfish are plentiful, these tiny crustaceans make up almost three-quarters of the smallmouth's diet. Other favorite smallmouth quarries are insects, tadpoles, shiner minnows, and various small fish. During periods of intense cold, the smallmouth bass lowers its metabolic rate and feeds very little if at all. As the water warms up in the spring, the fish go on a ravenous feeding spree just prior to spawning. During spawning, however, they don't eat at all. Food consumption reaches a peak as the water hits about 78°F (25°C). This is the time of year when food is plentiful and the metabolic rate of the bass is at its seasonal high. In the fall, as the water temperature drops, so does the appetite of the smallmouth bass, until, finally, the water dips below 40°F (4.5°C) and feeding ceases entirely.

The smallmouth relies primarily on its sense of sight for finding food. Therefore it is more likely to strike lures with a more natural look than those that appear artificial. The fish has an extremely sensitive lateral line and good hearing. It can easily pick up strange vibrations and noises in the water and will flee an area or cease feeding if it senses a threat. Biologists feel that the smallmouth's sense of smell is not very developed; however, many anglers swear by the effectiveness of scented lures. The wariness of the smallmouth depends on the overall bass population of its habitat. In waters where the population is low and food is plentiful, the fish is much more selective in its eating habits. If there is strong competition for food, the fish is more aggressive.

Because of their wariness and intense fighting ability, the smallmouth bass has become a favorite quarry for fly anglers.

The same spinning, bait-casting, and fly tackle that is used on the largemouth bass is effective for the smallmouth; however, because the smallmouth is slightly smaller, you can usually get away with slightly lighter tackle. The most popular outfit is a 5-to-6-foot (1- to 2-m), light- or medium-weight bait-casting rod, loaded with 6-to-10-pound- (3- to 5-kg) test line. In cool, clear northern streams, light- to medium-weight fly tackle is also very popular.

The smallmouth hits on a wide variety of surface and underwater plugs, spoons, spinners, jigs, plastic worms, bass bugs, and streamer flies designed for the largemouth. The lures used for a smallmouth, however, should be slightly smaller. Crawfish are easily the best natural bait. Other effective baits include hellgrammites, dead lamprey eels, salamanders, frogs, crickets, grasshoppers, and worms.

Early spring and fall are the best seasons for catching these tenacious fish. They stay in waters from 2 to 15 feet (.6 to 5 m) deep while actively searching for food. In the southern

In the summer, smallmouth bass move into waters from 15 to 40 feet (5 to 12 m) deep, usually around some sort of deep water structure. Look for them around the edges of cliffs, sharp drop-offs, and underwater islands.

© John Telford

portions of the fish's range, the spring season usually starts in March or April. Farther north the season may not begin until May or June. Spring feeding begins in earnest as the water reaches about 50°F (10°C). Overall, smallmouth populations have been on the decline in recent years. As a result, many areas prohibit fishing for these fish during their spawning season and have strictly limited the bag limits during the rest of the year. While the smallmouths are extremely tasty fish, they should be caught and released in order to keep fishing pressure at a minimum.

In the summer, smallmouths retreat into deeper waters and feed less actively. They generally hold in waters from 15 to 40 feet (5 to 12 m) deep. While occasionally they stay suspended in open water, for the most part smallmouths like to hold over or around some sort of deep-water structure. A few good spots to look for smallmouth bass include the edges of cliffs and sharp drop-offs, underwater islands, old underwater river beds, and the deep pools of a river.

© Gregory K. Scott/Nature Photos

Left: ***An angler prepares to land a good-sized fish. Smallmouths can put up an extremely strong fight for their size.*** **Right:** ***Fly fishing for smallmouths has become extremely popular over the past several years. Here an angler goes after bass in the Rum River, Minnesota.***

The most exciting and challenging angling for smallmouths takes place in cool, swift rivers and streams. River bass are much more wary and difficult to fool than those in lakes or reservoirs. As with fishing the perpetually skittish trout, you should approach bass streams with a great deal of caution. Avoid crashing through the brush and casting long shadows across the stream. Also, fish from the shore and avoid wading if possible. When fishing from a boat, approach sensitive fishing areas as quietly as possible. Use either oars or an electric motor. Stop the boat a good distance away and make long casts to the fishing hole.

In rivers or streams the smallmouths feed near the shore in shallow water, especially during the spring and fall. They like banks and sandbars that are usually above water, but have been flooded by spring rains. They search these areas for minnows, frogs, crawfish, and mayflies. Other hot spots include sharp bends or curves in a stream, and the deep sides of rock ledges. The fish can also be found

behind fallen trees and under overhanging banks. In addition, they will enter moderate rapids, riffles, and the quick water at the heads and tails of pools to search for bait fish.

In clear, calm water it is best to use light tackle with light lines and small lures to avoid spooking the fish. Small spoons are the most popular and effective lures for catching smallmouth bass. Cast the spoon across and upstream for the intended hole and let it sink to the bottom with the current. As the spoon begins flowing with the current, quickly raise the rod tip high to pull the spoon off the bottom, and then allow it to sink down again. Repeat this action so that the small spoon rises, sinks, and tumbles down the stream. Most strikes occur as the lure is sinking to the bottom, so be alert for any unusual tugs or pulls on your line.

Near right: ***An angler nets a smallmouth caught with a jig.*** **Far right:** ***A fly angler casts into the Snake River in central Minnesota.***

While jigs are probably the most effective lures for fishing the deep waters of lakes and reservoirs, they can serve equally well in streams and rivers. They are easy to use and produce a multitude of strikes. The best jigs for smallmouths are dark in color with black, brown, or gray feathers attached. Adding a strip of pork rind or a worm to the hook can significantly increase your strikes. Cast the jig just as you would a spoon, across and upstream, and let it drift with the current toward the fish. As it reaches the bass, begin retrieving it with slow, short pulls so that it imitates the action of a crawfish crawling along the bottom.

© Wally Eberhart

In lakes and reservoirs, smallmouths can be found in shallow areas and near the shore during the spring, early summer, and fall. Even in the middle of the summer, when they spend most of their time down deep, bass enter shallow areas in the early morning and late evening to feed. Look for them along rocky shores, craggy points that border deep water, offshore sandbars and shoals, underwater islands, and near ridges that border sharp drop-offs. Small, shallow underwater plugs are very effective for snagging bass when they are feeding in the shallow waters of lakes and reservoirs. Diving minnow plugs such as Rapala and Rebel are your best choice. Make a long cast from a boat or shoreline to the spot where the fish are holding. Begin a slow retrieve so that the lure wiggles and swims across the top of the water. Quickly increase the speed of your retrieve every few seconds so that the lure dives a few feet below the surface and then rises

© Greg L. Ryan/Positive Reflections, Inc.

Mad River Canoe

If you are unfamiliar with the waters you are fishing, it is a good idea to buy and study a topographical map of the area before doing any fishing. Expert anglers can take one look at a map and determine the most likely places to find fish, even if they've never been to that area before.

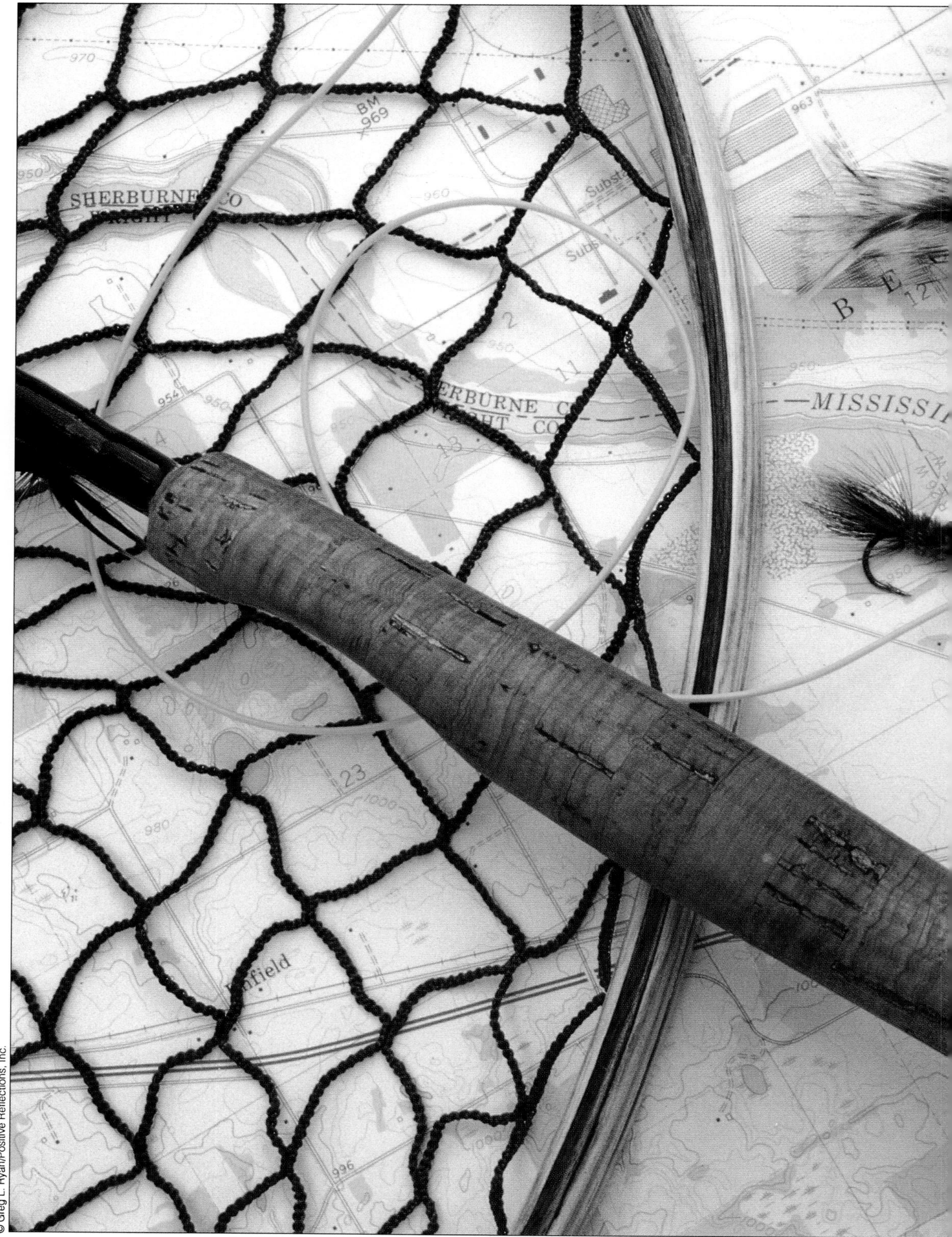

© Greg L. Ryan/Positive Reflections, Inc.

back up. If you know the fish are there but you aren't getting any strikes, it may just be that they are feeding closer to the bottom. In this case, if you switch to a deep-diving or sinking plug your luck may change.

In midsummer, when the bass have retreated to deeper water, trolling is the most effective method for locating and catching them. Use spinning or bait-casting tackle rigged with underwater plugs, spinners, spoons, jigs, or natural bait. Fly rods rigged with a streamer or bucktail fly can be very effective when the bass are in waters between 6 and 20 feet (2 and 6 m) deep. Vary your trolling speed and depth until you find out where the fish are located. In lakes, troll around jagged shorelines and over heavy structure. A topographical map of the lake or reservoir and an electronic depth finder are helpful tools for finding bass hot spots. In a large river, troll slowly upstream, taking care to cover all of the deep pools and coves where the bass may be holding.

After you locate the fish, use vertical jigging to pull them from deep

water. Use a small, short jig, weighing between $\frac{1}{16}$ and $\frac{3}{8}$ of an ounce (1.75 and 10.5 g). The amount of extra weight you need on your line will depend on the current of the water and the depth of the fish. Lower your jig over the edge of the boat and let it sink freely until it touches the bottom or hits the structure that the bass are holding around. Then begin raising and lowering the jig with long sweeps of your rod. Experiment with different depths and jig actions until you start to get strikes.

Once hooked, the smallmouth bass most certainly will put up a determined and tireless fight, especially in shallow water. The fish will usually make an initial charge downstream and then head for deep water. Never underestimate the smallmouth when playing it on the line. This fish has a great deal of stamina. Just when you think it is tired and ready to give up, it may make one last desperate run for freedom. Even though the smallmouth is smaller than the largemouth bass, it is definitely, pound for pound, a much stronger fighter.

Chapter 5

Courtesy U.S. Fish & Wildlife Service

Striped Bass

During the 1920s, '30s, and '40s, both state and federal governments in the United States began programs to harness the country's extensive river systems for hydro-electric power and irrigation. The rivers

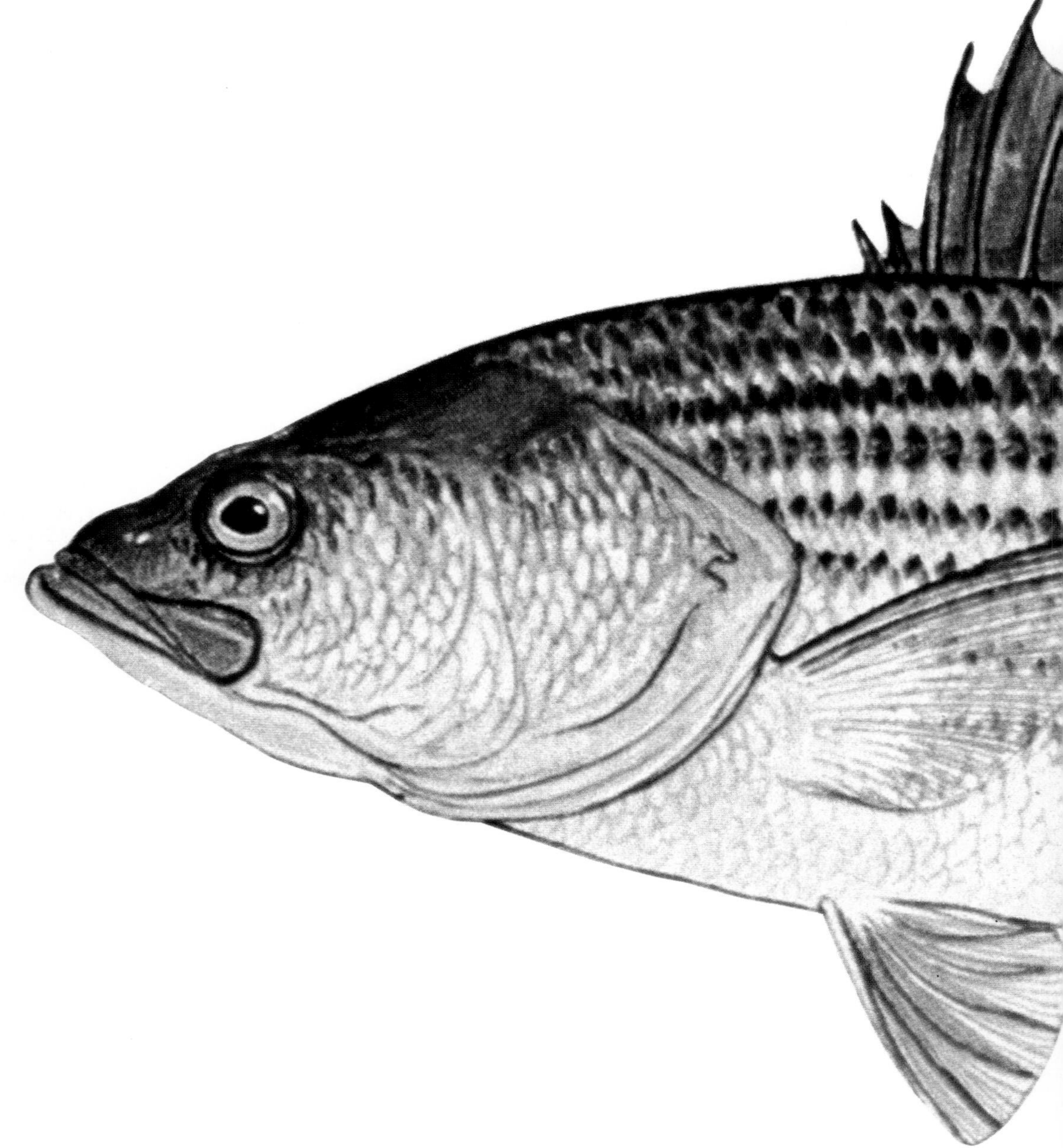

The striped bass, or* Morone saxitillis, *gets its common name from a series of six to nine longitudinal stripes on its upper sides.

represented a powerful source of energy for a country that had grown dramatically in the past one hundred years. Irrigation canals were built, dams were erected, and the courses of thousand-year-old rivers were altered. While most of these projects were necessary to help support the country's economic and energy needs, they were quite often planned and completed with little regard for their environmental impact. The salmon fisheries in Canada, the Pacific Northwest, and the northeastern United States are still reeling from irresponsible water-management policies.

In 1941, the state of South Carolina erected dams across the Santee and Cooper rivers, blocking off the spawning runs of the oceangoing striped bass. These dams unexpectedly created a new fishery in the United States. Many of the stripers were trapped in Lake Marion and Lake Moultrie—the two lakes created by the dams. These now landlocked fish thrived in the clean, warm waters of the newly created lakes. In fact, with ample supplies of gizzard shad, sculpin, shiners, and other bait fish, these freshwater stripers grew at a much faster rate than their saltwater counterparts. In the ocean, a striped bass takes ten to twelve years to reach a weight of 19 pounds (9 kg). In fresh water, however, the same species can grow by as much as 5 pounds (2 kg) per year, reaching a weight of 21 pounds (9 kg) in six years.

The striped bass, or *Morone saxitilis* is a moderately compressed, elongated fish with an olive-green to dark blue back, silvery sides, and a white belly. It gets its common name from a series of six to nine longitudinal

stripes on its upper sides. The oceangoing striped bass tends to be much darker than the landlocked variety, with an almost jet-black back, dark silvery sides, and a white belly. In addition, the stripes on the oceangoing variety are less pronounced. Other common names for *Morone saxitilis* include squidhound, linesides, greenhead, rockfish, and striper.

While fishing for landlocked stripers is a relatively new sport, anglers have been catching the oceangoing fish since the early seventeenth century. Both early white settlers and Native Americans in New England hooked or netted stripers on the stripers' spring spawning run. Many times, however, these fish were inadvertently caught while the anglers were fishing for Atlantic salmon and trout.

The original range of the striped bass includes the Atlantic Ocean and its associated rivers from the St.

© Gregory K. Scott/Nature Photos

An angler releases his catch back into the wild. Striped bass have been widely transplanted into rivers and lakes in the Mississippi River system, the Colorado River, and in coastal rivers and lakes in California, Oregon, and Washington.

Lawrence River to the St. Johns River in Florida, and along the Gulf Coast, from the Appalachicola River in West Florida to Lake Ponchartrain in Louisiana. The oceangoing fish is most abundant, however, from the Hudson River to the Chesapeake Bay. Stripers have been widely transplanted into rivers and lakes in most of the Mississippi river system, the Colorado River, and in coastal rivers in California, Oregon, and Washington.

In 1879, fishery biologist Livingston Stone and California fish commissioner Stephen Throckmorton arranged the transplant of nearly 200 small striped bass from the Navesink River in New Jersey to the Carquinez Strait near San Francisco Bay. This marked the first appearance of the striped bass on the Pacific Coast. A few years later they made another transplant to the lower Suisun Bay, also near San Francisco.

The two fishing experts could not have hoped for a more successful undertaking. From just these two small transplants a fishery of more than ten million stripers developed, and by the early 1990s the striped

© Frank S. Balthis/Nature's Design

Because of poor water management policies, the striped bass population in the western United States drastically dropped from ten million in the late 1880s to less than one million in 1985.

bass supported a major commercial fishing industry on the West Coast. At their peak, the transplanted stripers ranged from Monterey, California, to Oak Park, Washington.

Unfortunately, the California water-management policies of the early twentieth century wreaked havoc on the striped bass population. The extensive damming of rivers across California blocked the fish's spawning rivers, just as populations were booming. Millions of the fish depended on the delta and the upper reaches of the San Joaquin and Sacramento rivers for spawning. Federal and state water projects effectively cut off these spawning grounds reducing the West Coast striper population from ten million in the late 1880s to less than one million by 1985. Those fish that regularly spawned in the upper reaches of the rivers were forced to spawn in the delta. The eggs and tiny bass fry were then sucked through fish screens and intake pumps and distributed into the canals and lakes behind the dams, where they formed landlocked populations.

© Wally Eberhart

Like most other types of fish, striped bass do most of their feeding near sunrise or sunset, when the temperatures are relatively cool. This is the time when striped bass are most apt to surface feed.

The migratory striped bass has been more recently threatened by the illegal stocking of white bass in a few lakes that empty into the San Joaquin River. Biologists fear that if these fish make their way into the San Joaquin and then eventually the Sacramento River, they will hybridize with the oceangoing striped bass. Such hybridization could further devastate striped bass populations in the region. White bass/striped bass hybrids, known as whiterock bass, have been purposely stocked in many less sensitive, landlocked southern water systems with great success.

Fishing for landlocked striped bass has become immensely popular over the past several years. Anglers have enthusiastically accepted this relatively new game fish to the point that it now nearly equals traditional largemouth and smallmouth bass fishing in terms of popularity. Stripers are relatively large for freshwater fish, generally weighing between 5 and 20 pounds (2 and 9 kg) in most waters, although 30- and 40-pounders (15- and 18-kg) are fairly common in the Deep South. In

Courtesy Eppinger

***At left** is a variety of terrestrials for bass and trout including: Devil Bug Mouse, Midget Trout Bug, Trout Devil Bug, Bass Devil Bug, and Winged Bass Bug. **Below:** Two men jig for striped bass on Lake Almanor, California.*

1977, Frank Smith set a freshwater record when he pulled a 59-pound, 12-ounce (27-kg, 336-g) striper from the Colorado River, near Bullhead City, Arizona.

While the striped bass reproduces naturally in the rivers and streams feeding certain lakes, most landlocked populations have to be periodically restocked by fishery officials. They normally spawn in the spring when water temperatures reach 61° to 69°F (16° and 21°C). A single 10-pound (5-kg) female can produce over a million eggs at spawning time; however, very few landlocked settings are conducive to striper reproduction—the Santee/Cooper river system in South Carolina, the Lake Havasu/Colorado river system in Arizona, and Lake Meade in Nevada all have the necessary conditions for spawning.

The striped bass has adapted a freshwater diet of gizzard shad, threadfin shad, large shiners, staghorn sculpin, riffle sculpin, and silversides, any of which can be used as a natural bait. Striped bass travel in large schools like their close relatives the white bass. In a typical lake, they cover many miles a day searching for schools of bait fish. The hungry stripers surround the bait fish and herd them into a cove or bay, or trap them against some sort of structure. Once their quarry is cornered, the stripers begin a frenzied, frothy surface slaughter, which will no doubt attract the interest of hungry gulls and eager anglers.

The tackle for catching striped bass is basically the same as that used for largemouth or smallmouth bass, pike muskellunge, coho or chinook salmon, lake trout, or any other large freshwater fish. The most popular outfit is a 5½-to-6-foot (1.6- to 2-m) medium-weight bait-casting rod and reel, loaded with about 200 yards (180m) of 6-to-10-pound- (3- to 4.5-kg-) test monofilament line. The

Some anglers use heavy saltwater-type equipment for catching stripers, particularly when deep-trolling; however, fishing with lighter equipment makes for much better sport.

action of the rod should be stiff enough to allow for long casts and provide enough backbone to pull the strong, large stripers out of the water. Of course, the size and weight of your outfit will depend largely upon the size of the fish you are catching. In lakes where they abound, stripers tend to be a bit smaller because of the heightened competition for food. For the best sport, you should use the lightest tackle possible to pull in your catch. This will, of course, depend on your personal preferences and angling ability.

© Dick Dietrich

Many anglers like to use heavy salmon fly rods for hauling in stripers. When fishing from the shore in areas where long casts are necessary (near the tailwaters of dams and falls, for example), it may be necessary to use a long, two-handed spinning rod similar to the saltwater outfits used for surf casting. Some of these rods are as long as 10 or 12 feet (3 or 3.6 m) and can hurl a bait or lure quite a distance. If you are deep-water trolling for stripers, you may need a heavy bait-casting or trolling rod loaded with wire-core line in order to reach the proper depths. The best sport in deep-water trolling, however, is had by using relatively light tackle and a downrigger to get your lure down deep. It is easy to control your depth with a downrigger, and you will have more fun battling the bass with light tackle.

Striped bass are not very particular about the look of a lure, especially during their frenzied surface feeding. If it looks anything like a swim-

© Don Johnston/Photo/Nats

In the spring, stripers will head into tributary streams and rivers to spawn. Even after the spawning season has ended, the fish will often remain in these tributaries to forage for small shad and other bait fish.

ming or injured bait fish, they hit it eagerly. They are, however, particular about the size of the lure. Carry several sizes of lures in your tackle box and try to closely match the size of your lure with the bait fish the stripers are eating. The same types of surface and underwater plugs, spoons, spinners, jigs, streamer flies, and plastic lures you use for black bass will work for stripers.

Shad is the favorite food of the striped bass, and is therefore the best natural bait to use. Either gizzard shad or threadfin shad will do, and they can be fished either alive or dead. Other good natural baits include freshwater herring, alewives, needlefish, waterdogs, small eels, panfish, and large minnows. Many anglers claim great success using dead saltwater baits such as anchovies, herring, and sardines.

Striper season begins in the early spring and lasts through late fall. In some southern waters good fishing can be had year-round, although striper activity usually slows down during the midwinter and midsummer months. Where to locate the fish,

In early spring, striped bass will move into shallow water areas to spawn and feed. This is when striper fishing is at its best. Look for stripers in the fast tailwaters of dams, falls, or other obstructions. Here an angler fly casts for striped bass, while, opposite page, *two anglers search the banks from a canoe.*

© Greg L. Ryan/Sally A. Beyer/Positive Reflections, Inc.

and the fishing technique to use to catch them depends largely on the time of year, the weather, and the time of day you will be fishing. In early spring, stripers will begin moving upstream to spawn. The spawning run can occur as early as February and March in the South, and as late as May or June farther north.

Spring fishing offers some of the best striper action all year. The fish will be in shallow water and extremely hungry. Look for them in the fast tailwaters of dams, falls, or other obstructions blocking their spawning run. They will gather there and forage on a multitude of bait fish while looking for a way upstream. If the turbines of the dam are turned on, you should be in for some especially good fishing. The turbines will spew out injured or stunned bait fish from the other side of the dam, directly into the mouths of the hungry stripers. The stripers will strike at virtually anything that resembles a vulnerable bait fish. Sometimes the tailwaters can be so dense with stripers that their tails and fins will be flapping and churning the surface of the water. When

© Saul Mayer

they are feeding on top, you may want to use a surface plug such as a popper, chugger, swimmer, or a crippled minnow propeller lure; however, a simple spoon is just as effective and easier to use in swift water. Striped bass can be easily frightened in their feeding frenzy, so keep your distance and make long casts to the area you are fishing. Cast up and across stream from the spot where they are feeding, and let your lure tumble and swing toward the fish. If the water is moving swiftly enough, you need no action on the lure. Otherwise, you may want to try lifting and lowering your rod in a herky-jerky motion that will make your lure resemble an injured bait fish.

In rivers and streams, stripers tend to feed on the surface during the early morning or evening hours, and sometimes late at night. These are the best times to catch them. However, if you are fishing in late morning or during the afternoon, or if it is a particularly hot, sunny day, the fish may be feeding on or close to the bottom. In these situations you will have to put your surface plugs away and rig up an underwater plug, spoon, spinner, or jig. Jigs are most effective when the fish are down deep in relatively swift currents. Cast upstream and across and let the jig sink to the bottom. The current will bounce the jig along the bottom and, hopefully, swing it into the mouth of a hungry striper. In fast currents it may be nec-

© Robert A. Walsh

© Hank Andrews/Visuals Unlimited

Above: *When striped bass are surface feeding in schools, the fishing can be fast and furious. It is essential to have a swift boat in order to get to the feeding schools before they go below the surface.* Left: *In contrast to hectic spot fishing, this angler spends a lazy morning jigging from a bridge.*

essary to add a little weight to your line in order to get it deep enough. Be careful not to allow too much slack on your line, otherwise you won't be able to set the hook.

When they are not feeding on the surface, striped bass often hold near some sort of structure. Hot spots include bends in the stream or river, sandbars, points, shoals bordering deep water, bridges, overhanging trees, and large boulders or rock piles. In large rivers these hot spots may be difficult to cast to from shore. Use a long, two-handed spinning rod if you have to cast over great distances.

Many anglers like to fish for stripers with a fly rod in streams and small rivers. The best fly for this situation is a large streamer or bucktail. Remember that the size of the fly should closely match the size of the bait fish the stripers are feeding on. Here again, cast across and upstream and allow the fly to swing down with the current to the fish. If you don't get a strike by the end of the swing, begin slowly retrieving the lure in short jerks. Periodically let the fly drift back downstream a few feet and then begin

Opposite page: ***An angler battles a striper as the sun sets across the lake.***

retrieving again. The idea here is to imitate the movements of an injured bait fish or minnow. A striper is more likely to go after an injured fish than one that appears healthy.

Yet another way to fish for stripers in a river is from a small boat. Drift the boat along jagged points, sandbars, and drop-offs near deep water. Do not get too close to the hot spots, or you might startle the fish. Instead, drift about 50 feet (15 m) away and cast to the fish. It is best to use a row boat, canoe, or small boat with an electric motor. Gasoline motors are too noisy and will scare the fish.

The most exciting striper fishing comes when the fish are chasing schools of shad or other small fish on the surface of lakes. This usually occurs in the early morning or evening in the spring or fall. As stated earlier in this chapter, schools of striped bass will surround and attack schools of bait fish in a water-churning outburst of relentless feeding. The attacks may last only a few seconds or for as long as five or ten minutes. Many anglers who know their striper waters well can fairly accurately predict when and where these feeding displays will take place. This "jump," or "spot," fishing, as it is known, requires a swift boat, a keen eye, and many prerigged rods at the ready.

Scan the sky for circling gulls, often a sign that a school of bait fish is near the surface. The water surface will churn with activity as the stripers begin the attack. You must be quick in getting your boat over to the feeding, because you never know how long the frenzy will last. As you approach the school, shut off your engine and let the boat drift into position. Do not speed too close to the school or you will put the bass down before you can cast a single lure. To avoid wasting time rigging rods or switching lures, have two or three extra rods rigged with different lures

Courtesy U.S. Fish & Wildlife Service

Clockwise from top left: ***Mepps Agua French Spinner, Cotton Cordell Pencil Popper, Hula Popper, Rapala Swimming Plug, Mr. Twister, and Crazy Crawler.*** **Opposite page:** ***An angler fly fishes from a canoe on Lake Ascot, Wisconsin.***

at the ready. Make long casts to the fish, using surface lures such as poppers, torpedoes, chuggers, propeller spinners, and swimmers. Work the lures quickly, making a lot of commotion on the surface. You will most likely reel in fish as fast as you can cast. Many times, just the smaller members of the school are making all the commotion on the surface. The larger ones may be feeding from just below the surface to as deep as 20 feet (6 m). Because of this, you should have at least one extra rod rigged with an underwater plug, jig, or spoon. Simply cast to the fish and quickly reel the lure back in. There is no need to put any action on the rod, as the fish will be biting at anything that swims.

In large lakes and reservoirs it is often difficult to locate the schools of stripers. Like the *white bass*, they move around the body of water looking for bait fish, sometimes covering seven to ten miles a day. If you are unfamiliar with the lake you are fish-

© Greg L. Ryan/Sally A. Beyer/Positive Reflections, Inc.

ing, ask local fishery officials, marina and tackle shop owners, and local anglers for advice. While they may keep the best spots to themselves, they will often be helpful in pointing you in the right direction. Also, while you are on the lookout for gulls and schools of bait fish, keep an eye on the other anglers on the lake, you can often learn more from a fisherman's actions than from his words.

During midsummer and midwinter, surface feeding will drastically slow down. Occasionally there will be good jump fishing in the early morning and late evening; however, you generally have to go down deep to find the stripers. Most of the time they will be suspended in water from 15 to 40 feet (5 to 12 m) deep. An electronic depth finder or fish finder is essential for locating the fish when they are down deep. Like largemouth bass, stripers will hold near unusual underwater structure at lower depths. Look for them near underwater stream beds, steep ledges and drop-offs,

When fishing for striped bass from shore, pay particular attention to rocky points and jutting sandbars. Also, keep an eye out for schools of bait fish, especially young shad.

© Dick Dietrich

flooded roadbeds, deep-water shoals, and old bridge abutments. Most marinas sell topographical maps of lakes and reservoirs. Pick one up and study it for potential hot spots.

The key to finding striped bass in the summer is finding the schools of bait fish they forage on. Early in the morning, stripers congregate around the entrances to coves and bays as well as the mouths of tributary rivers, in hopes of running into a school of migrating shad. Fish these areas well in the morning, paying particular attention to rocky points and jutting sandbars that border on deep water. At other times of the day, use your depth finder or fish finder to locate schools of bait fish and, in turn, striped bass.

If you don't have the luxury of an electronic fish finder, trolling is a good method for locating stripers, because it enables you to cover a lot of water in a short amount of time. For trolling you will need heavier tackle than for casting. The best outfit is a heavy, freshwater, bait-casting rod, filled with 15- to 20-pound- (7- to 9-kg-) test monofilament line. If you are trolling

© Robert A. Walsh

Striped bass will readily go after live bait such as minnows or shiners. In many areas, however, it is illegal to fish with non-indigenous minnows because they can upset the natural fish population.

deeper than about 40 feet (12 m), you will need a wire-core line if you don't have the aid of a downrigger.

Once you locate the fish, vertical jigging is the best method to use for pulling them from the deep. Use a rigid bait-casting, rod and reel loaded with 15- or 20-pound- (7- or 9-kg-) test monofilament line. Heavy spoons, such as Kastmaster, Topo, Dardevle, Little Cleo, and Hopkins seem to be effective for vertical jigging. Many times adding a small shiner or minnow to the hook of your jig will increase your luck.

The stripers usually hold around or just over some sort of structure, such as a sandbar, rock pile, shoal, or drop-off. Drift your boat over the area and let your lure sink freely until it hits the bottom. Most strikes come as the lure is sinking, so be alert for any hits. Begin raising and lowering your rod tip in wide sweeps to give the lure a jerky up-and-down motion. Gradually raise the depth of the lure until you determine exactly where the fish are holding. They may be right on the bottom, directly over some sort of structure, or suspended somewhere

An angler fishes for migrating striped bass at sunset.

© Bob Firth/Firth Photobank

between the surface and lake floor. Once you locate the fish, mark your line and keep fishing that depth until you stop getting strikes. Then either experiment with different depths again, or move on to another area. When the water is extremely cold or extremely warm, the stripers will be very inactive, and less likely to hit a swift-moving lure. If this is the case, experiment with different actions, making shorter, less energetic sweeps, or moving the rod tip from side to side instead of up and down.

While vertical jigging is not nearly as quick or exciting as spot fishing or shore casting at the foot of a dam, you can nonetheless catch your fill of big, tasty striped bass. In the South striped bass fishing is usually good throughout the year, and even in the North the season is quite long, sometimes lasting into November or December. The future looks bright for this relatively new freshwater game fish sport. Every year, more and more anglers try their hand at hauling in these big hawgs, and stocking programs place them in new waters.

Chapter 6

© Carl Hanninen/Photo/Nats

WHITE BASS

It's a warm spring morning on the Watts Bar Reservoir in Tennessee. The water is calm, the sun is bright, and the reservoir is dotted with small boats carrying two or three anglers apiece. The anglers are

Also known as the sand bass or silver bass, the white bass usually has an olive-gray back and distinctive white or silvery sides.

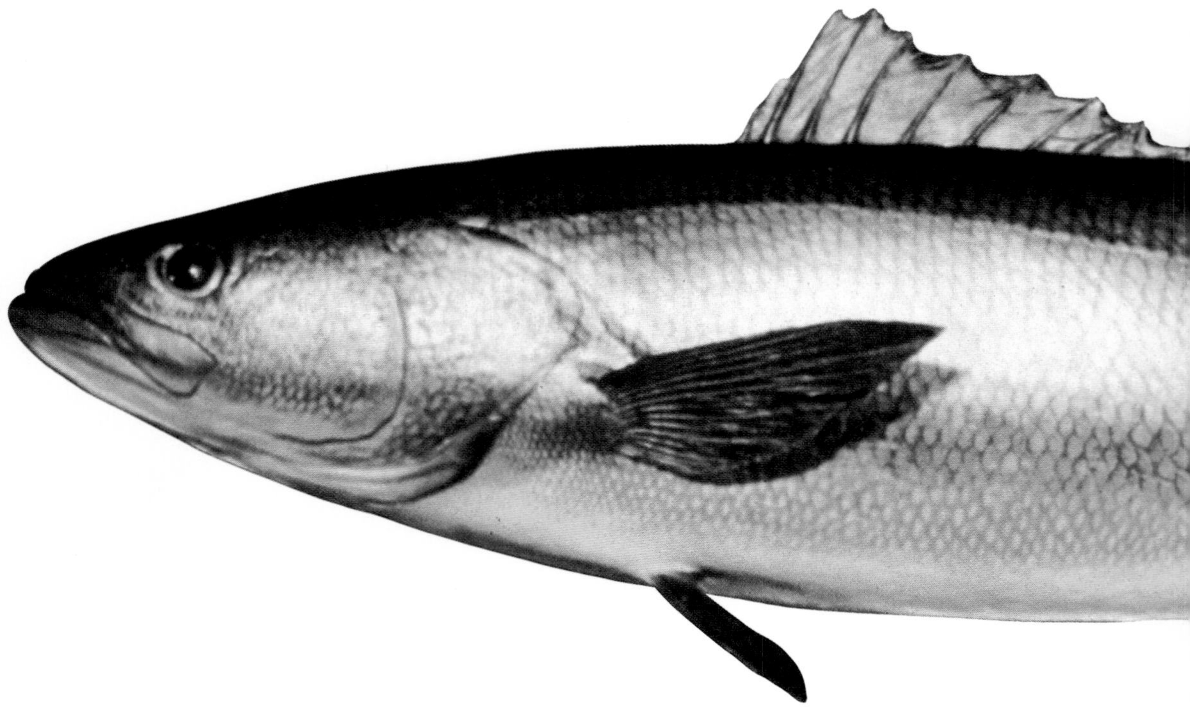

searching the sky for circling gulls or terns. They then shift their attention to the water, looking for signs of bait-fish schools or the telltale surface disturbance of a feeding frenzy. A few anglers spot some circling gulls a couple hundred yards down the lake. The water below the gulls is pocked with ripples and splashes. The anglers immediately start up their boats and begin heading toward the disturbance. As they approach, the water begins churning. There is a hungry school of white bass relentlessly feeding on a school of gizzard shad. The anglers drift into position and begin casting their lines and pulling in fish as fast as they can. The fishing is frenzied as the anglers try to bag as many fish as they can while the bass remain on the surface. In a few minutes the school disappears below the surface and the anglers scan the sky and the water again for signs of the next rise.

"Jump," or "spot," fishing for white bass is an extremely exciting and rewarding form of angling. The schools of fish can appear and disappear in a few minutes. The angler must be alert and ready at any moment to zero in on the catch.

The natural range of the white bass includes Lake Winnipeg, the St. Lawrence River, the Great Lakes, the Mississippi river system, New Mexico, and the lakes and rivers along the Gulf Coast, from Louisiana to Texas. It is, however, an extremely prolific fish that has been successfully transplanted throughout the United States, especially in the Southeast and Southwest. Whites thrive in man-made lakes and reservoirs connected to large river systems. Unlike the largemouth and the smallmouth bass, whites very rarely seek any type of cover. They travel in large schools and prefer relatively clear water with sand, rock, or gravel bottoms. While they feed on the surface and enter shallow water to spawn, white bass spend most of their time in water from 15 to 30 feet (5 to 9 m) deep.

The white bass, or *Morone chrysops,* is a member of the "temperate basses," or the family Percichthy-

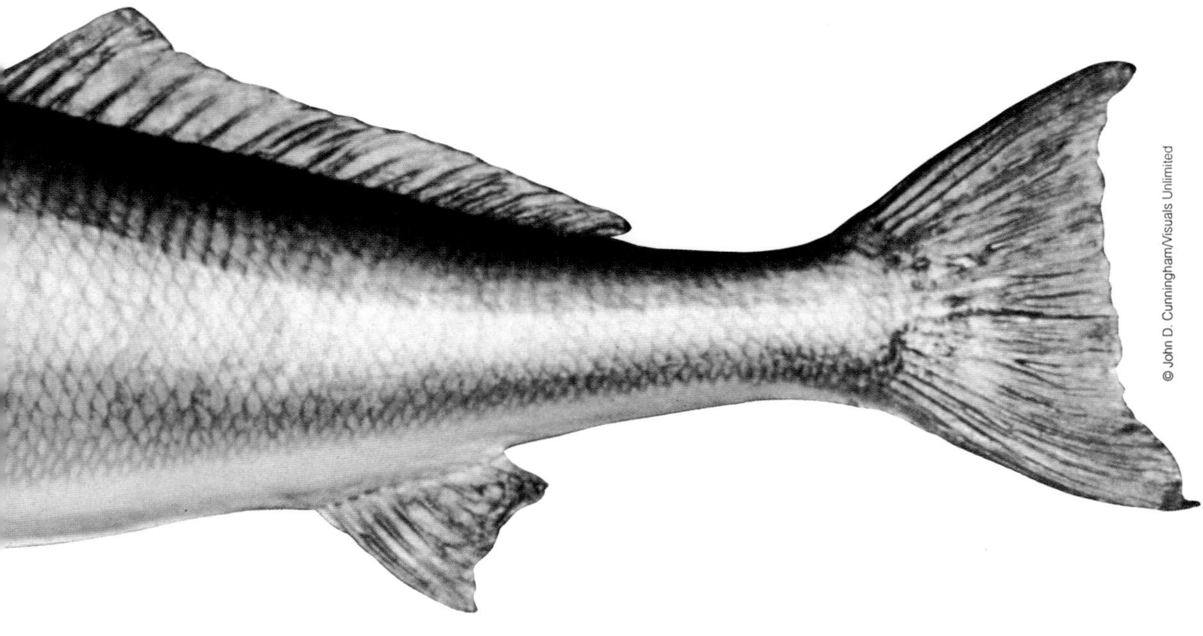

idae, and is not directly related to the largemouth or smallmouth bass. Other North American members of this group include the white perch, the yellow bass, and the striped bass. These fish are all characterized by one or two opercular spines, a complete lateral line that extends to a forked caudal fin, and two completely separate dorsal fins.

Other names for the *Morone chrysops* include the sand bass, silver bass, barfish, and gray bass. In some areas, it is also known as the striped bass or striper. This moniker, however, confuses the white bass with its freshwater/saltwater relative *Morone saxatilis,* the true striped bass. The white bass is a laterally compressed fish with an olive to olive-gray back, silver to white sides with dark stripes, and a yellowish belly. It has a protruding lower jaw and a mouth that extends to the middle of the eye.

Several years ago, white bass populations were illegally transplanted into a few lakes that empty into the San Joaquin River. Biologists fear that if these fish make their way into the San Joaquin and eventually the Sacramento River, they will hybridize with the oceangoing striped bass. Such hybridization could potentially devastate striped bass populations in the region. White bass that were legally introduced into environmentally sound areas of California have done very well, creating a new and very popular fishery for California anglers.

White bass/striped bass hybrids, known as whiterock bass, have been purposely stocked in many less sensitive, landlocked, southern water systems. This cross between a female striped bass and a male white bass is larger and more aggressive than the pure white bass and has the potential to develop into an exciting new game fish.

The best fishing for white bass is in the southern United States, especially in the man-made lakes and reservoirs of Texas and the Tennessee Valley. Because of the longer growing season, southern white bass are more plentiful and usually a bit larger than northern whites. While extremely

© Jeff Greenberg

Prime White Bass Waters

Texas	Buchanan Lake, Caddo Lake, Colorado River, Livingstone Lake, Marshall Lake, Pedernales River, the Rio Grande, Sulpher Lake, Texoma Lake, and Travis Lake
Tennessee	Center Hill Lake, Douglas Lake, Kentucky Lake, Pickwick Lake, Watts Bar Reservoir, and virtually any lake or reservoir in the Tennessee Valley Authority
Kentucky	Buckhorn Lake, Dale Hollow Lake, Dewey Lake, Dix River, Herrington Lake, Kentucky Lake, Lake Barkley, Lake Cumberland, Nolin Lake, and the Rockcastle River
South Carolina	Catawba River, Clark Hill Reservoir, Lake Greenwood, Lake Hartwell, Lake Murray, and the Savannah River
Wisconsin	Lake Mendota, Lake Monona, Lake Winnebago, Lake Wonona, Wisconsin River, and the Wolf River

Man-made lakes and reservoirs such as those of the Tennessee Valley Authority provide the perfect conditions for the proliferation of white bass.

© Jeff Greenberg

fast-growing fish—they may reach 1 pound (.5 kg) after just two years—white bass seldom get very big, because of their short life span. Most whites only live for two to four years, with a few making it to the ripe old age of six. Most anglers pull in whites weighing between 3/4 and 2 pounds (.3 and .9 kg). In Texas, 4- or 5-pounders (2- or 2.5-kg) are occasionally pulled in, but this is extremely rare. The rod-and-reel record for the white bass is a 5-pound, 14-ounce (2-kg, 392-g) fish pulled in from Kerr Lake, North Carolina, in 1986.

White bass spawn in the spring in tributary streams of large lakes and reservoirs, after the water reaches 60°F (16°C). In southern regions, spawning starts as early as March or April; in the North it can be as late as May or June. Unlike largemouth and smallmouth bass, whites do not build nests. The female releases her eggs—sometimes more than half a million—over a gravel or rock bottom. The male simultaneously releases his milt and fertilizes the eggs as they sink to the bottom. In reservoirs or lakes with no accessible tributaries, the fish simply move into shallow water to spawn.

The eggs hatch within twenty-four to forty-eight hours, and the small fry immediately form dense schools for protection. This schooling instinct remains with the white bass their entire lives. They usually travel in groups of hundreds or even thousands of fish. Like many other fish species, white bass school by size. So if you are catching nothing but small bass, you may want to move to another area and search for a school of larger fish. White bass schools are constantly on the move, sometimes covering up to ten miles a day.

Spawning time is the peak season for white bass fishing. During this time, the fish are very aggressive, easy to find, and will strike at just about anything. While angling for many other species of fish is frowned upon by the general angling public, angling for spawning white bass is not. These fish are so plentiful and so prolific, and their life span is so short, that even heavy fishing during the spawning season will not harm the overall fish population.

SOUTHERN

Courtesy U.S. Fish & Wildlife Service

© John Telford

A few hot spots for white bass include large pools, inlets, riffles, still waters behind rocks, and slow eddies at the bases of dams or waterfalls.

The spring fishing season actually begins a few weeks before spawning begins. As the water temperature reaches the low fifties, white bass start migrating upstream. As they move upstream, the fish stop periodically to rest in slow-current areas such as large pools, eddies, inlets, riffles, and still waters behind rocks and boulders. They move into their spawning grounds as the water approaches 60°F (16°C). Sections of these streams can be so thick with white bass that the water will seem to boil with activity. Hot spots are slow eddies at the base of dams or waterfalls, behind log jams and fallen trees, and slow-current areas near the edges of swift rapids. The spawning season only lasts for a few weeks, so the bass will remain in shallow water for another few weeks afterwards. Look for them at the mouths of tributary streams, above sandy or gravelly shoals, near old, underwater stream beds, and again at the feet of dams and falls.

Courtesy G-Loomis, inset photo © Layne Messing

A 5½ to 6 foot (1.5 to 2 m), light- to medium-weight spinning or bait-casting rod, loaded with 4- to 6-pound- (2- to 3-kg-) test line is the outfit of choice for fishing white bass. These relatively small fish go after light lures, so be sure your outfit is light enough to cast the proper lures.

The best outfit for catching white bass is a light 5½- to 6-foot (1.6- to 2-m) freshwater spinning rod and a lightweight reel loaded with 4- to 6-pound- (2- to 3-kg-) test line. The lighter the tackle you use, the more fight you will get from the white bass, and the more enjoyable the fishing will be. Many ultralight outfits are even suitable for white bass. Bait-casting equipment is also suitable for white bass; however, be sure it is light enough to effectively cast the light lures needed for catching whites.

While white bass are not very picky as to what type or shape of lure they will hit, they are very particular about the size of the lure. These fish have relatively small mouths and will not usually hit any lure larger than ½ ounce (14 g). It is important to match your lure size with the size of the food the bass are eating on a particular day. Even when your lure doesn't closely resemble the fish's natural food in color or appearance, it may still be effective if it is about the same size as the natural food.

Shad is the favorite food of white bass. While the majority of shad hatch in the spring and then grow as the summer progresses, some shad hatch throughout the summer. As a result, the only sure way of knowing what size fish the bass are eating is through observation. White bass may feed on older, more fully developed shad one day and switch to small, recently hatched shad the next. Keep an eye out for shad and other bait fish and try to match your lure size to them as closely as you can. Just as the plastic worm is the best all-around lure for the largemouth bass, the jig is the most effective lure for the white bass. When white bass are in shallow water in the spring or when they are down deep in the summer, jigs can be crawled or bumped along the bottom. When the fish are feeding on the top, jigs can be cranked across the surface of the water. For the most part, white bass will go after a fast-

© Alissa Crandall

moving lure rather than a slow one. This is especially true when they are feeding in open water.

Many of the techniques recommended for striped bass fishing can be applied to white bass fishing. In late spring and early summer, white bass feed in large packs. Like striped bass, these fish hunt down and corner large schools of bait fish, force them to the surface, and then begin a relentless feeding attack. These feeding sprees may last anywhere from forty-five seconds to several minutes. If you are lucky enough or quick enough to locate such surface activity, you will no doubt be able to catch fish as fast as you can cast. It is a good idea to have one or two extra rods at hand, rigged with different-size lures. Once the feeding begins you don't want to waste time rigging up your line. White bass have razor-sharp gill covers that can very easily cut your line. Check it frequently for nicks and scrapes. Even the slightest wear may cause your line to snap at the most inopportune moment.

There is no surefire way of determining exactly when or where these feeding sprees may take place. Keep an eye out for schools of bait fish, surface disturbances, and circling gulls, all signs that a feeding spree is about to occur. Once you locate a school of surface-feeding bass, get to that spot

Below: *When midsummer comes and the fish go deep into the lake, vertical jigging is one of the best methods for catching white bass. Here is a variety of walking jig set ups by Cabela.* Right: *A pair of anglers jig for white bass at sunset.*

as quickly as possible. As you approach the school, cut your motor and drift into position. White bass are very skittish. The sound of a loud outboard motor or the clink of gear being dropped on bottom of the boat may startle the fish and force them back underwater.

As midsummer sets in and the water temperature rises, white bass feed less and less on the surface, and, as a result, are increasingly harder to find. In fact, at the height of the summer, white bass may stay as deep as 40 or 50 feet (12 or 15 m). When this occurs, a depth finder or fish finder is essential to angling success. This device wil help you locate schools of bait fish, or the white bass themselves. If you don't have such an electronic device, trolling is the best way to locate the fish. Remember to vary your trolling speed and depth until you find just the right combination. White bass tend to hit lures trolled at speeds much greater than other types of fish. Some anglers have great success trolling for whites at speeds as high as 6 to 8 miles (10 to 12 km) per hour.

Vertical jigging is another very effective way of pulling whites out of deep water. Jig from a drifting boat, rather than an anchored one, until you locate a school of bass. Then anchor and fish until that area ceases to be productive. Here again, a small but heavy jigging spoon is your best choice of lure. Let it sink to the bottom, and then begin to work it up and down with short jerks of the line. Most hits will come as the lure is sinking, so be alert for even the slightest changes in your line.

The white bass puts up a remarkably good fight for its size, especially when hooked on light tackle. Once hooked, it will dive for deep water, jerk from side to side, and make fairly long runs for a panfish. White bass almost never breach, however. Even when hooked on the surface, they will immediately dive far below to do their fighting.

The popularity of white bass fishing has been steadily increasing over the past several years. They are very prolific fish that can withstand the heaviest of fishing pressure. While the expert angler may not find a great deal of challenge in these small fish, they are, nonetheless, a very good fish for the novice or intermediate angler.

Courtesy Cabela's

© Wally Eberhart

BIBLIOGRAPHY AND RECOMMENDED READING

The Audubon Society, *The Audubon Society Field Guide to North American Fishes, Whales, and Dolphins.* New York: Alfred A. Knopf, 1983.

Bergman, Ray, edited by Edward C. Janes, *Fishing with Ray Bergman.* New York: Alfred A. Knopf, Inc., 1976.

Evanoff, Vlad, *The Freshwater Fisherman's Bible.* New York: Doubleday, 1980.

Ginrich, Arnold, *The Well-Tempered Angler.* New York: Plume, 1987.

Hackle, Sparse Grey, *Fishless Days, Angling Nights.* New York: Fireside Books/Simon & Schuster, 1988.

Haig-Brown, Roderick L., *A River Never Sleeps.* New York: Crown Publishers, 1974.

Leiser, Eric, *The Book of Fly Patterns.* New York: Knopf, 1977.

Lyons, Nick, *Bright Rivers.* New York: Fireside Books/Simon & Schuster, 1977.

Lyons, Nick, *The Seasonable Angler.* New York: Fireside Books/Simon & Schuster, 1988.

Maclean, Norman, *A River Runs Through It.* Chicago: University of Chicago Press, 1983.

Marinaro, Vince. *In the Ring of the Rise.* New York: Nick Lyons Books, 1976.

Rosenthal, Mike, *North America's Freshwater Fishing Book.* New York: Scribner, 1984.

Schaffner, Herbert, *The Fishing Tackle Catalog: A Sourcebook for the Well-Equipped Angler.* New York: Gallery Books, 1989.

Schaffner, Herbert, *Freshwater Game Fish of North America.* New York: Gallery Books/W.H. Smith Publishers, 1989.

Schullery, Paul, *American Fly Fishing: A History.* New York: Nick Lyons Books, 1987.

Schultz, Ken, *Bass Fishing Fundamentals.* New York: Stephen Green Press/Viking, 1987.

Soucie, Gary, *Soucie's Fishing Databook: Essential Facts for Better Fresh & Saltwater Fishing.* New York: Winchester Press, 1985.

Taylor, Nick, *Bass Wars.* New York: McGraw-Hill, 1987.

Woolner, Frank and Hal Lyman, *Striped Bass Fishing.* New York: Nick Lyons Books, 1985.

Index